GRADE
2

SCHOLASTIC

Reading & Math

This book belongs to

_____

Cover design by Sequel Creative
Cover art by Patrick Girouard
Interior illustrations by Maxie Chambliss, The Everett Collection, New York, James Graham Hale, Greg Harris, Mark Mason, Sherry Neidigh, Karen Sevaly, and Carol Tiernon

ISBN 0-439-78601-0

17 16 15 14 13 12 11   08   14 15 16

Dear Parents,

The power to succeed is in every child! The question is: How can you help your child achieve this success and become an independent, lifelong learner?

You have already taken the first step! *Reading & Math* is the perfect way to support the learning your child needs to be successful in school.

Research shows that independent practice helps children gain mastery of essential skills. This book includes carefully selected, teacher-tested activities that give second graders exactly the practice they need. Topics covered include:

- Phonics
- Spelling
- Cursive Writing
- Vocabulary
- Addition, Subtraction, and Multiplication
- Time, Money, and Measurement

You'll also find assessments to help you keep track of your child's progress—and provide important practice with standardized test formats.

Let's get started! Your involvement will make this a valuable educational experience and will support and enhance your child's learning.

Enjoy!

Hindie

Hindie Weissman
Educational Consultant,
27+ years teaching experience

GRADE 2 — Learn and Succeed

Welcome to *Reading & Math!*

Grade 2 is a critical stepping stone on the road to learning success! This workbook has been carefully designed to help ensure your child has the tools he or she needs to soar in school. On the 300-plus pages that follow, you'll find plenty of practice in each of these must-know curriculum areas:

CURSIVE ALPHABET	PHONICS/SPELLING	READING SKILLS	VOCABULARY
• Writing Letters • Copying Sentences	• Recognizing Short & Long Vowel Spellings • Understanding Digraphs & Diphthongs • Recognizing Unusual Vowel Sounds • Spelling List	• Recognizing Main Idea/Details • Recognizing Cause/Effect • Using Context Clues • Comparing & Contrasting • Analyzing Characters	• Understanding Synonyms, Antonyms, Homonyms, & Homophones • Recognizing Compound Words • Learning Content Area Words • Understanding Analogies
GRAMMAR	**WRITING**	**NUMBERS**	**MATH CONCEPTS**
• Recognizing Types of Sentences • Understanding Parts of Speech	• Sentence Building • Understanding Parts of a Story • Subject/Verb Agreement • Using Punctuation	• Understanding Addition • Understanding Subtraction • Understanding Multiplication	• Understanding Time • Understanding Money • Understanding Measurement

Helping your child build essential skills is easy!

These teacher-approved activities have been specially developed to make learning both accessible and enjoyable. On each page, you'll find:

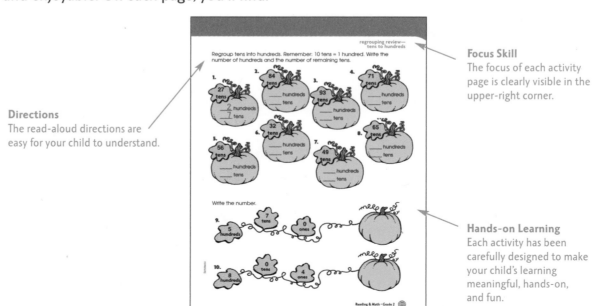

Directions
The read-aloud directions are easy for your child to understand.

Focus Skill
The focus of each activity page is clearly visible in the upper-right corner.

Hands-on Learning
Each activity has been carefully designed to make your child's learning meaningful, hands-on, and fun.

Scholastic

with Reading & Math!

These great extras are guaranteed to make learning extra engaging!

Reading & Math is loaded with lots of motivating, special components including:

SPECIAL ACTIVITIES TO GET READY FOR THIRD GRADE ▶

Give your child a head start in third grade with this BONUS assortment of get-ready activities.

◀ CONNECTION TO ONLINE LEARNING

Boost computer literacy with this special link to a treasury of skill-building online activities at www.scholastic.com/success.

MOTIVATING STICKERS ▶

Mark the milestones of your child's learning path with these bright, kid-pleasing stickers.

◀ INSTANT FLASH CARDS

Promote reading fluency with these fun flash cards.

REWARD CERTIFICATE ▶

Celebrate your child's leap in learning with this colorful, pull-out completion certificate.

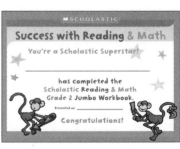

◀ LIST OF THE BEST BOOKS FOR YOUNG LEARNERS

Reinforce key concepts and build a love of reading with this great list of learning-rich books selected by top educators. See page 12.

QUICK ASSESSMENT TESTS ▶

Make sure your child *really* masters each must-know skill with the instant assessment tests that conclude each section.

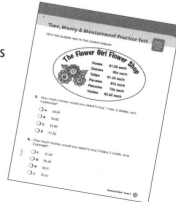

Table of Contents

Scholastic

Scholastic

MATHEMATICS

Scholastic

Tips for Success

Here are some tips to help your child get the most out of this workbook:

- Provide a quiet, comfortable place for your child to work.

- Make sure your child understands the directions.

- Encourage your child to use colorful pencils and markers to make learning fun.

- Check completed work as soon as possible and review corrected work with your child.

- Pay attention to areas where your child is having difficulty. Spend extra time to help him or her master those skills.

- Provide a special area at home where your child's work can be displayed.

- Be positive and encouraging. Praise your child for his or her efforts and good work.

Scholastic

Read with Your Child

Reading to your child and having him or her read to you is an extremely effective way of supporting your child's learning. When you read with him or her, make sure your child is actively participating. Here are five ways to support your child's reading:

1. Let your child choose the book.

2. Look at the cover of the book and ask your child what he or she thinks the story will be about.

3. As you read the book, locate a good stopping point and ask your child to predict what will happen next. Then read to confirm the prediction or correct it.

4. Discuss the characters in the story: Are they kind? good? bad? clever? Are they like characters in another book?

5. When you finish the story, have your child retell it.

Read with Your Child

Looking for a great book to read to your child? Here are some top teacher picks:

- *Alexander and the Terrible, Horrible, No Good, Very Bad Day* by Judith Viorst (Aladdin, 1987).

- *Horrible Harry in Room 2B* by Suzy Kline (Puffin, 1997).

- *The Littles* by John Peterson (Little Apple, 1993).

- *The Man Who Walked Between the Towers* by Mordicai Gerstein (Roaring Brook, 2003).

- *Miss Nelson Is Missing!* by Harry Allard (Houghton Mifflin, 1985).

- *Olivia* by Ian Falconer (Atheneum, 2000).

- *Rhema's Journey* by Ifeoma Onyefulu (Scholastic, 1990).

- *Second-Grade Friends* by Miriam Cohen (Scholastic, 1993).

- *The True Story of the Three Little Pigs* by Jon Scieszka (Puffin, 1996).

- *Mufaro's Beautiful Daughters: An African Tale* retold by John Steptoe (HarperTrophy, 1993).

The Alphabet in Cursive

Learning to write in cursive brings a delightful sense of "I'm growing up!" to your child. In this section, children transfer their knowledge of letters and the sounds they make from manuscript handwriting to the cursive alphabet.

What to Do
Have your child use pen, pencil, or markers on the letter writing practice pages to trace and write the letters. Then have your child write the words and the sentence in cursive. When finished, invite him or her to circle their "best" upper- and lowercase letters.

Keep On Going!
Encourage your child to use cursive handwriting to write invitations, thank-you notes, or friendly letters to friends and family members.

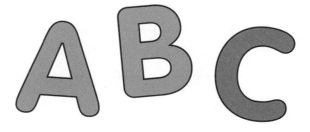

A a

Trace and write.

a a a a a

a a a a

a a a a

Austin Av

ant   arid

Al and Ann act

in Australia.

B b

Trace and write.

B B

b b

B b

Boise

bib   baby

Bob bakes brownies

in Bakersfield.

Cc

Trace and write.

C C

c c

Cc

Chicago

city   cute

Christy and Celia

chat in Cancun.

Scholastic

Dd

Trace and write.

D D

d d

Dd

Denver

did   dot

Didi and Dad

dive in Dallas.

E e

Trace and write.

E E

e e

E e

Eugene

eye   each

Emma encountered

Ethan in Egypt.

$\mathcal{F}f$

Trace and write.

$\mathcal{F}$ $\mathcal{F}$

f f

$\mathcal{F}f$

Freeport

fife   file

Frankie frees Fifi

from a fight.

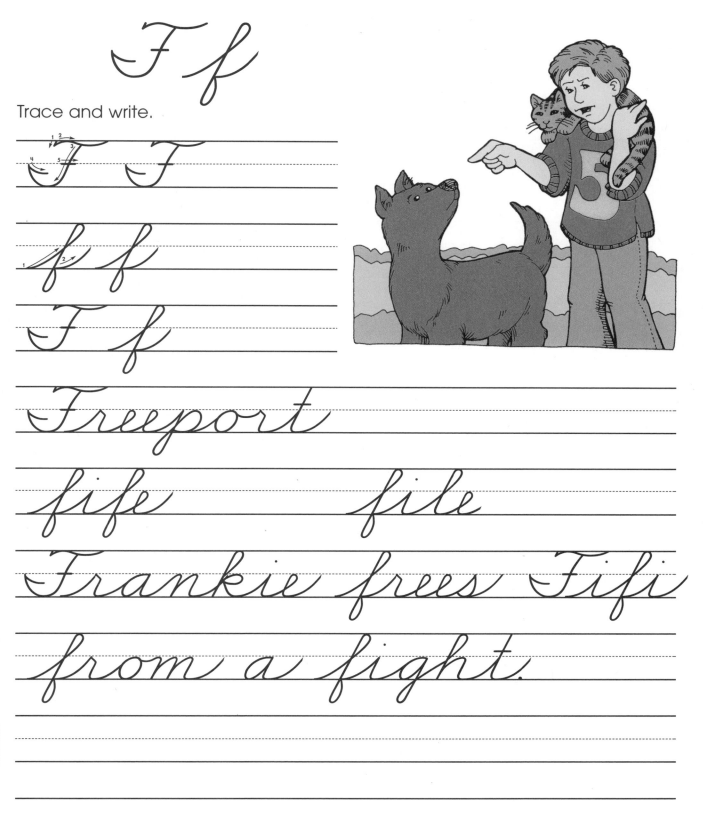

Gg

Trace and write.

G G G

g g g

Gg

Glendale

goat   gig

Gabi goes to Greece

to greet Grandpa.

Hh

Trace and write.

H H

h h h

H h

Honolulu

high   hat

Honey, the hamster,

hides in the hedge.

Ii

Trace and write.

L L L

it it

Ii

Ionia

into   ink

Ida itches in

Indianapolis.

J J j

Trace and write.

J J

J j

J J j

Joliet

jolt   *jest*

Jay jumps over

Jack and Jessica.

K k

Trace and write.

K K

k k

K k

Kent

kite   keep

King Kirk kicks

in Kenya.

L l

Trace and write.

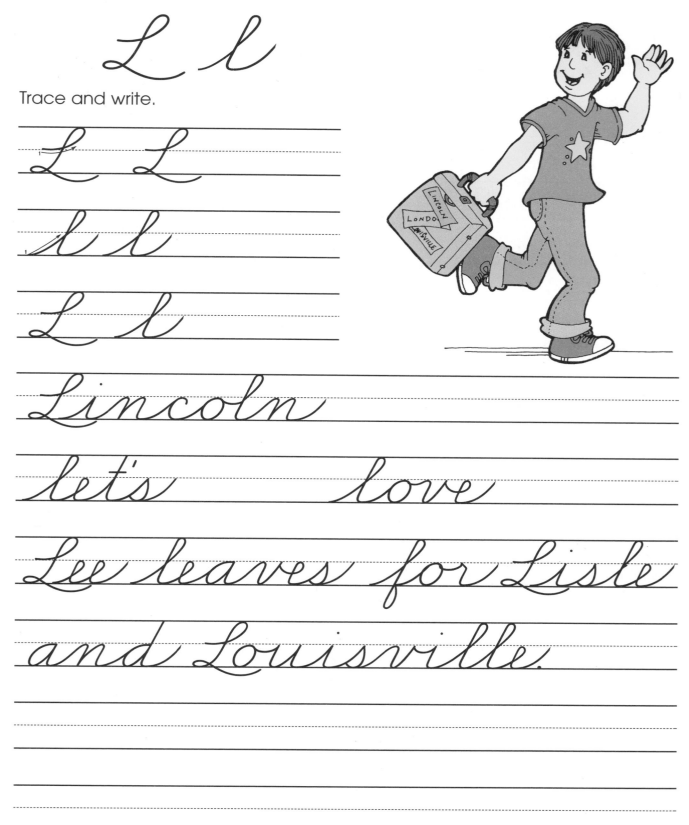

L L

l l

L l

Lincoln

let's   love

Lee leaves for Lisle

and Louisville.

M m

Trace and write.

M M

m m m

M m

Memphis

mom   map

Mia met Mick on

Monday in Mexico.

Nn

Trace and write.

Nn

m n

Nn

Norwalk

noon   not

Nate nibbles nuts

in New Mexico.

Oo

Trace and write.

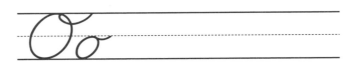

Olympia

onto   *oil*

Oli and Otis order

Oregon oranges.

Scholastic

Pp

Trace and write.

P P

p p

Pp

Peoria

pipe   pot

Peg plays piano

in Pittsburgh.

$\mathcal{Q}\ q$

Trace and write.

$\mathcal{Q}\ \mathcal{Q}$

$q\ q$

$\mathcal{Q}\ q$

Quincy

quiz   quit

Queen Quia quilts

quietly in Quebec.

Scholastic

R r

Trace and write.

R R

r r

R r

Reno

roar   rare

Rob rests in Rome

and in Richmond.

Ss

Trace and write.

St. Louis

sail   sit

Sam and Susan

sing in Seattle.

Tt

Trace and write.

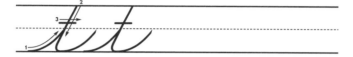

Tt

Tucson

tot   tip

Tita and Timmy

tan in Tahiti.

$\mathscr{U}u$

Trace and write.

$\mathscr{U}\mathscr{U}$

$\mathscr{u}\ \mathscr{u}$

$\mathscr{U}u$

$\mathscr{U}rbana$

up $utter$

$\mathscr{U}ri\ used\ a\ ukelele$

$in\ \mathscr{U}zbekistan.$

$\mathcal{V}\,v$

Trace and write.

$\mathcal{V}\,\mathcal{V}$

$v\,\,v$

$\mathcal{V}\,v$

Ventura

vase   vote

Vince volunteered

to visit Venezuela.

Ww

Trace and write.

W W

w w

Ww

Westover

wow   wit

Wendy saw Wesley

in Washington, D.C.

Scholastic

$\mathcal{X}\mathit{x}$

Trace and write.

$\mathcal{X}\,\mathcal{X}$

$\mathit{x}\,\mathit{x}$

$\mathcal{X}\mathit{x}$

$\mathcal{X}\mathit{enia}$

$\mathcal{X}\text{-}\mathit{ray} \qquad\qquad \mathit{fox}$

$\mathcal{X}\mathit{avier}\ \mathit{exited}\ \mathit{with}$

$\mathit{six}\ \mathit{xylophones.}$

Y y

Trace and write.

Y Y

y y

Y y

Yakima

yard   yet

Yetta and Yuri

visit Yellowstone.

$\mathcal{Z}\ z$

Trace and write.

$\mathcal{Z}\ z$

$\mathcal{Z}\ z$

$\mathcal{Z}\ z$

Zenda

zip   zero

Zeb zigzagged from

Zambia to Zaire.

Cursive Alphabet Practice Test

Fill in the bubble next to the correct answer.

Example

Which letter is missing?

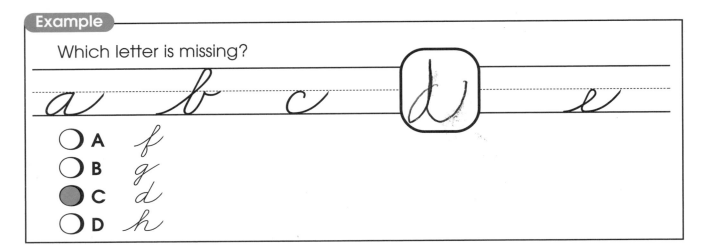

- ○ **A** f
- ○ **B** g
- ● **C** d
- ○ **D** h

---

1. Which letter is missing?

- ● **A** g
- ○ **B** l
- ○ **C** o
- ○ **D** m

---

2. Which letters are missing?

- ○ **F** r, s, t
- ○ **G** r, u, w
- ○ **H** $q, r, s,$
- ○ **J** p, r, u

Scholastic

Cursive Alphabet Practice Test

Choose a sticker to place here.

Fill in the bubble next to the correct answer.

3. Which word would come first in a dictionary?

○ **A** *orange*

○ **B** *apple*

○ **C** *fruit*

○ **D** *banana*

4. Which word would come last in a dictionary?

○ **F** *green*

○ **G** *blue*

○ **H** *red*

○ **J** *white*

5. Which word would come after the letter h in a dictionary?

○ **A** *high*

○ **B** *glad*

○ **C** *jump*

○ **D** *ice*

Scholastic

Phonics/Spelling

"Look, Mom, I can read it all by myself!" What a proud moment for your child. Understanding the relationship between letters and the sounds they make is the most important step in learning how to read. In this section, children use their knowledge of phonics to develop spelling skills.

What to Do

These activities provide practice in the spelling of rhyming words, vowel and consonant sounds, and unusual spellings of certain sounds.

Read the definition of the skill to your child. Then have him or her complete the activity. Help your child check the work when finished. Answers, if needed, are provided in the back of the workbook.

Keep On Going!

Play a word game with your child. Tell him or her, I am thinking of a word:

>It starts with a *k* sound.
>It has a short-*a* in the middle.
>It ends with a *t* sound.
>It rhymes with *fat*.
>What is the word? [*cat*]
>How do you spell it?

The rows in each parking lot contain words that rhyme, going across.
Write the words in the empty spaces to show where the incoming cars
should park.

bead

let

shake

seed	knead	reed
snake	bake	rake
wet	let	fret

there	Where	hair
ground	round	sound
tramp	Stamp	lamp

wear

camp

found

brush

ate

should

would	mould	could
rate	date	skate
brush	flush	slush

The **short-*a* sound** *is found in the word* **map**.

A. Read and copy each list word. Circle the letter that makes the short-*a* sound. Watch for a word with an unexpected silent-*e* ending. Then organize the list words by their number of letters.

List Words

1. map
2. ask
3. last
4. has
5. sack
6. clap
7. after
8. mask
9. black
10. have

1. m a p
2. a s k
3. _____
4. _____
5. _____
6. _____
7. _____
8. _____
9. _____
10. _____

three letters

m a p
_____
_____

five letters

_____
_____

four letters

_____
_____
_____
_____
_____

Challenge Words

11. backpack
12. stamp
13. stand

11. _____
12. _____
13. _____

B. Change one letter in each word to spell a list word. The first one has been done for you.

1. ash ___ask___
2. mash _____
3. slap _____
4. block _____
5. list _____
6. lap _____
7. his _____
8. sick _____
9. hive _____

A. Use the list words to complete the story.

Matt's Map

Matt _has_ a map of the houses on his street. He keeps the map in his _mask_ sack. _last_ night Matt could not find his map. He looked everywhere. "Do you _have_ my map?" he would _ask_ everyone. Matt saw something under his Halloween _sack_ It was his _map_ Matt was so happy he began to _clap_. _after_ that, Matt always put his map back in his black _sack_.

B. Follow the clues to play tic-tac-toe. As you find each answer, mark an *X* or *O*. Do you get three in a row?

1. I am the antonym (opposite) for *answer*. Mark an *X*.
2. I am a color. Mark an *O*.
3. I rhyme with *past*. Mark an *X*.
4. I am the antonym for *before*. Mark an *O*.
5. She _____ a sister. Mark an *X*.
6. I begin like the word *sit*. Mark an *O*.
7. I rhyme with *map*. Mark an *X*.
8. They _____ a dog. Mark an *O*.
9. I rhyme with *ask*. Mark an *X*.

has	have	clap
black	mask	sack
last	after	ask

Write the challenge word that finishes each analogy.

10. You put a plate on the table. You put a _____ on a letter.
11. *Down* is the antonym for *up*. *Sit* is the antonym for _____.
12. A wallet is kept in a purse. A book is kept in a _____.

The **short-e sound** *is found in the word* **tent**.

A. Read and copy each list word. Circle the letter that makes the short-*e* sound. Watch for a word with an unexpected spelling. Then organize the list words by their ending letters.

 List Words

				words that end with *t*	words that end with *d*
1.	tent	1.	_____		
2.	met	2.	_____	_____	_____
3.	send	3.	_____	_____	_____
4.	went	4.	_____	_____	_____
5.	bed	5.	_____	_____	_____
6.	nest	6.	_____	_____	_____
7.	bend	7.	_____	_____	
8.	yet	8.	_____	_____	
9.	best	9.	_____		
10.	said	10.	_____		

Challenge Words

11. bench   11. _____
12. next   12. _____
13. else   13. _____

B. Each list word has a rhyming partner. Write two list words that rhyme.

1. _____   2. _____   3. _____
   _____   _____   _____

4. _____   5. _____
   _____   _____

Circle ten misspelled words. Write them correctly on the lines.

My Backyard Tent

My dad and I built a (tint) in the backyard.
We had to bind sticks to stake it in the
ground. We had the beste time. We made
a bid out of straw. We sed it was like a bird's
nast. My mom said she would sind a snack
out to us. We mete her in the yard and then she whent back in the house.
She said she isn't ready for camping yat!

1. tent   2. _____   3. _____   4. _____

5. _____   6. _____   7. _____   8. _____

9. _____   10. _____

Use addition and subtraction to spell each list word. The first one has been done for you.

11. rest – r + b = ____best____

12. test – s + n = _____

13. mat – a + e = _____

14. bad – a + e = _____

15. sent – t + d = _____

16. sand – n + i = _____

17. send – s + b = _____

18. set – s + y = _____

19. next – x + s = _____

20. want – a + e = _____

Write the challenge word that matches each definition.

21. another choice _____

22. a place to sit _____

23. the nearest in order _____

*The **short-i sound** is found in the word **miss**.*

A. Read and copy each list word. Circle the letter that makes the short-*i* sound. Then organize the list words by the letter clues.

List Words

1. hid
2. mix
3. with
4. tip
5. milk
6. miss
7. slip
8. kick
9. kiss
10. pick

1. _____
2. _____
3. _____
4. _____
5. _____
6. _____
7. _____
8. _____
9. _____
10. _____

words that begin with *m*

_____

_____

_____

words that have a *p*

_____

_____

_____

words that begin with *k*

_____

_____

words that have an *h*

_____

_____

Challenge Words

11. into
12. trick
13. sister

11. _____
12. _____
13. _____

B. Circle the word that is spelled correctly.

1. pik   pick
2. melk   milk
3. kiss   kis

4. tip   tipp
5. slep   slip
6. kik   kick

7. hid   hidd
8. miks   mix
9. mis   miss

Scholastic

Write the list word that matches each clue.

1. I am the past tense of *hide*. I am _____.

2. We rhyme with *sick*. We are _____ and _____.

3. I am part of the dairy food group. I am _____.

4. I begin with the same sound as *wind*. I am _____.

5. I am a synonym for *stir*. I am _____.

6. We rhyme with *flip*. We are _____ and _____.

7. Do this to your mom or dad. I am _____.

8. I am kiss – k + m. I am _____.

Circle each list word hidden in the puzzle. The words go across, down, or diagonally.

g	m	i	l	k	a	j	l	p	w	e	i	c	e	o
u	s	o	x	f	x	c	q	b	i	w	f	e	y	z
f	l	e	d	m	i	b	t	n	r	c	j	o	d	w
p	i	k	i	c	k	p	r	b	m	m	k	i	f	i
l	p	i	k	x	a	d	v	c	i	m	i	r	g	t
k	u	t	b	d	h	i	d	m	s	r	j	x	n	h
v	t	i	p	v	m	g	r	b	s	i	d	i	i	d
h	d	i	r	p	n	p	z	k	i	s	s	e	q	i
b	c	f	h	a	q	r	t	p	k	a	c	s	h	e

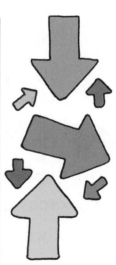

Write the challenge word that finishes each question.

9. Does Josie's _____ share a bedroom with her?

10. Did you stir the milk _____ the cake mix?

11. Have you learned a new magic _____?

The **short-*o* sound** *is found in the word* **sock**.

A. Read and copy each list word. Circle the letter that makes the short-*o* sound. Then organize the list words in rhyming pairs.

 List Words

1. sock	**1.** _____	_____	_____
2. mop	**2.** _____		
3. box	**3.** _____	_____	_____
4. spot	**4.** _____		
5. odd	**5.** _____	_____	_____
6. off	**6.** _____	_____	_____
7. dot	**7.** _____		
8. stop	**8.** _____		
9. fox	**9.** _____		
10. lock	**10.** _____		

Which two words do not have a rhyming partner?

_____ _____

🏆 **Challenge Words**

11. clock   **11.** _____

12. cross   **12.** _____

13. stomp   **13.** _____

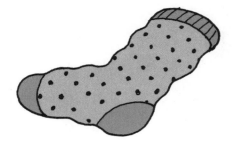

B. 👓 Change the vowel in each word to spell a list word.

1. map _____

2. step _____

3. sack _____

4. fix _____

5. lick _____

6. spit _____

7. add _____

Scholastic

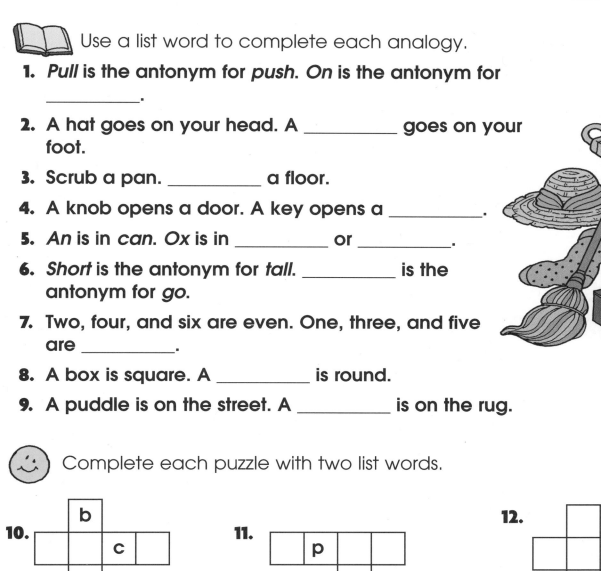

📖 Use a list word to complete each analogy.

1. *Pull* is the antonym for *push*. *On* is the antonym for _____.

2. A hat goes on your head. A _____ goes on your foot.

3. Scrub a pan. _____ a floor.

4. A knob opens a door. A key opens a _____.

5. *An* is in *can*. *Ox* is in _____ or _____.

6. *Short* is the antonym for *tall*. _____ is the antonym for *go*.

7. Two, four, and six are even. One, three, and five are _____.

8. A box is square. A _____ is round.

9. A puddle is on the street. A _____ is on the rug.

😊 Complete each puzzle with two list words.

10. | | b | | |
    | | | c | |

11. | | p | |
    | | f |
    | |

12. | |
    | | | k |
    | x |

13. | |
    | |
    | d | | |

14. | |
    | t | |
    | p |

⭐ Write each challenge word three times.

_____   _____   _____

_____   _____   _____

_____   _____   _____

Scholastic

The **short-u sound** *is found in the word* **bump**.

A. Read and copy each list word. Circle the letter that makes the short-*u* sound. Watch for words that use unexpected spellings. Then organize the list by the letters making the short-*u* sound.

List Words   *u*   *a*

1. rub   1. _____   _____   _____

2. bump   2. _____   _____

3. come   3. _____   _____   *o*

4. was   4. _____   _____   _____

5. dump   5. _____   _____

6. must   6. _____   _____

7. from   7. _____

8. dust   8. _____   *o_e*

9. tub   9. _____   _____

10. some   10. _____   _____

Challenge Words

11. lunch   11. _____

12. stuck   12. _____

13. stung   13. _____

B. Write a list word that begins with the same sound as the picture.

1. _____   2.  _____   3.  _____

4.  _____   5.  _____   6.  _____

7.  _____   8.  _____   *and*    _____

Use two list words to make a rhyme.

1. We hit a _____ on our way to the _____.

2. Will you give my back a _____ while I sit in the warm _____?

3. Achoo! I really _____ begin to _____.

4. These cookies are great! When I _____, I will bring _____.

Use the clues to identify the list words. Move the jeeps along the road by circling the answers. The jeep that reaches the end of the road first is the winner!

5. more than one

6. the past tense of *is*

7. a verb that rhymes with *cub*

8. starts like *friend*

9. jump – j + d

10. dirt

11. Change the vowel in *most*.

12. starts like *candy*

13. a noun that rhymes with *cub*

14. a _____ in the road

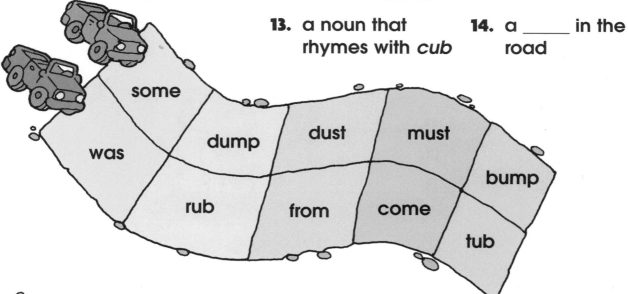

some
was
dump
dust
must
rub
from
come
bump
tub

Draw a picture to show each challenge word. Label the picture.

Each of these words has a short-vowel spelling with one final consonant. Before adding an ending like -ing or -ed, double the final consonant.

A. Read and copy each list word. Circle the letter that makes the short-vowel sound. Underline the words with double consonants.

 List Words

1. tap
2. tapping
3. beg
4. begged
5. skip
6. skipping
7. drop
8. dropped
9. run
10. running

🏆 **Challenge Words**

11. clapped
12. tripped
13. stopping

1. _____
2. _____
3. _____
4. _____
5. _____
6. _____
7. _____
8. _____
9. _____
10. _____

11. _____
12. _____
13. _____

words with no ending
_____
_____
_____
_____
_____
_____

words with an -ed ending
_____
_____

words with an -ing ending
_____
_____
_____

B. 👀 Unscramble the letters to spell the list words.

1. nunigrn _____
2. dgebge _____
3. propedd _____
4. spik _____
5. snigippk _____
6. patnpig _____

Scholastic

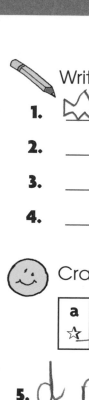 Write four sentences using at least two list words in each.

1. _____

2. _____

3. _____

4. _____

Crack the code to spell each list word.

a	b	d	e	g	i	k	n	o	p	r	s	t	u
☆	✧	✓	☉	✹	✪	⏰	★	⇧	✕	⧗	□	❊

5. d r o p p e d
   ✓ ✕ ⇧ ○ ○ ☉ ✓

6. ___ ___ ___ ___
   ⧗ ⏰ ✪ ○

7. ___ ___ ___ ___ ___ ___ ___ ___
   ⧗ ⏰ ✪ ○ ○ ✪ ★ ✹

8. ___ ___ ___
   ✕ ❊ ★

9. ___ ___ ___ ___ ___ ___ ___
   ✕ ❊ ★ ★ ✪ ★ ✹

10. ___ ___ ___ ___
    ✓ ✕ ⇧ ○

11. ___ ___ ___
    □ ☆ ○

12. ___ ___ ___ ___ ___ ___ ___
    □ ☆ ○ ○ ✪ ★ ✹

13. ___ ___ ___ ___ ___ ___
    ✧ ☉ ✹ ✹ ☉ ✓

14. ___ ___ ___
    ✧ ☉ ✹

 Write the challenge word that belongs in each group.

clap, clapping,	stop, stopped,	trip, tripping,

Scholastic

The **long-*a* sound** *can be spelled with the letters* a_e, ai *, or* ay.

A. Read and copy each list word. Circle the letters that make the long-*a* sound. Watch for a word with an unexpected spelling. Then organize the list words by the letters making the long-*a* sound.

List Words

		a_e	ai
1. say	1. _____	_____	_____
2. made	2. _____	_____	_____
3. snake	3. _____	_____	_____
4. pain	4. _____	_____	
5. away	5. _____		**ay**
6. trade	6. _____	**unexpected**	_____
7. train	7. _____	**spelling**	_____
8. brake	8. _____	_____	
9. trail	9. _____		
10. they	10. _____		

Challenge Words

11. raise	11. _____
12. plate	12. _____
13. scrape	13. _____

B. Write three list words that rhyme with one another.

1. _____   _____   _____

Six other list words have a rhyming partner. Write them below.

2. _____   3. _____   4. _____

_____   _____   _____

Scholastic

Use the list words to complete the letter.

Dear John,

My family went _____ for vacation. We took a _____ to Arizona. My favorite part was riding horses. We followed a _____ into the desert. Suddenly my horse had to _____. He saw a _____ on the trail. The snake was hurt and in _____. I didn't know what to _____. "Stop!" I called. The others _____ their horses stop. _____ saw the snake, too. We used a stick to move the snake under a rock. I hope he'll be okay.

Your friend,
Joe

P.S. Do you want to _____ baseball cards?

Follow the clues to complete the puzzle.

Across

2. rhymes with *sale*
3. to speak
6. a form of transportation
8. a synonym for *swap*
9. the past tense of *make*

Down

1. feel this when you are hurt
2. a list word with an unexpected spelling
4. rhymes with *day*
5. a reptile
7. a synonym for *stop*

Write the challenge word that finishes each analogy.

1. Lower is to move down as _____ is to move up.
2. Cut is to finger as _____ is to knee.
3. Drink is to cup as eat is to _____.

The **long-*e* sound** *can be spelled with the letters* e_e, *ea, or* ee.

A. Read and copy each list word. Circle the letters that make the long-*e* sound. Then organize the list words by the letters making the long-*e* sound.

List Words

			e_e	ee
1. meet	**1.** _____	_____	_____
2. each	**2.** _____	_____	_____
3. here	**3.** _____		_____
4. read	**4.** _____	*ea*	_____
5. seen	**5.** _____	_____	
6. team	**6.** _____	_____	
7. wheel	**7.** _____	_____	
8. mean	**8.** _____	_____	
9. eve	**9.** _____		
10. sleep	**10.** _____		

Challenge Words

11. these   **11.** _____

12. easy   **12.** _____

13. please   **13.** _____

B. Change one letter in each word to spell a list word. The first one has been done for you.

1. sheep_____*sleep*_____   **2.** been_____   **3.** melt _____

4. meal_____   **5.** tear _____   **6.** road _____

7. hare _____   **8.** ewe _____

Change the first and last letters to spell a list word.

9. sheet _____

10. back _____

Scholastic

Circle ten misspelled words. Write them correctly on the lines below.

A Sleepy Team

Last weak our gymnastics teem met heer. Eech boy and girl had to practice harder than before. We worked as hard as a hamster running on a weel. We did not even have a chance to sleap. At first we thought our coach was meen, but now I have sean what extra work can do for our team. We are all tired, but we are ready for our first gymnastics meet on New Year's Eev. You can rede about it in the newspaper. I hope we do well!

1. _____
2. _____
3. _____
4. _____
5. _____
6. _____
7. _____
8. _____
9. _____
10. _____

 Use addition and subtraction to spell each list word.

11. swan − sw + me = _____
12. sell − ll + en = _____
13. help − lp + re = _____
14. she − sh + ev = _____
15. rest − st + ad = _____
16. creep − cr + sl = _____
17. wheat − at + el = _____
18. well − ll + ek = _____
19. itch − it + ea = _____
20. clam − cl + te = _____

Write the challenge word that matches each definition.

21. simple _____

22. used with a request, to show good manners _____

23. used before a plural noun _____

The **long-*i* sound** *can be spelled with the letters* i_e, igh, *or* y.

A. Read and copy each list word. Circle the letters that make the long-*i* sound. Watch for a word that has an unexpected spelling. Then organize the list words by the letters making the long-*i* sound.

 List Words

1. sky
2. time
3. right
4. night
5. cry
6. wide
7. try
8. light
9. slide
10. why

	i_e	y
1. _____	_____	_____
2. _____	_____	_____
3. _____	_____	_____
4. _____		_____
5. _____	*igh*	
6. _____	_____	
7. _____	_____	
8. _____	_____	
9. _____		
10. _____		

Challenge Words

11. while
12. bright
13. stripe

11. _____
12. _____
13. _____

B. Circle the word that is spelled correctly.

1.	slyde	slide	2.	try	trie	3.	nite	night
4.	right	ryte	5.	skye	sky	6.	light	lite
7.	wide	wyde	8.	cry	crie	9.	whi	why

Scholastic

Write the list word that matches each clue.

1. I am the antonym for *day*. I am _____.

2. Children sit on me at the park. I am a _____.

3. I begin with the same sound as *truck*. I am _____.

4. I am used to ask a question. I am _____.

5. I am a synonym for *weep*. I am _____.

6. I am an antonym for *narrow*. I am _____.

7. We rhyme with *bite*. We are _____, _____ and _____.

8. I am always above you. I am the _____.

9. I tell past, present, and future. I am _____.

Circle each list word hidden in the puzzle. The words go across, down, or diagonally.

a	q	w	t	s	l	i	d	e	c	r
t	t	r	i	d	j	i	s	s	k	w
r	p	i	e	d	i	u	g	b	k	h
y	l	g	m	y	e	w	o	h	i	y
m	f	h	v	e	n	i	g	h	t	s
i	n	t	i	l	h	t	g	c	r	y

Write the challenge word that finishes each sentence.

10. My teacher said, "The American flag has 13 _____s."

11. "Did it rain _____ you were at the beach?" she asked.

12. Michael shouted, "I have a _____ idea!"

Scholastic

The **long-*o* sound** *can be spelled with the letters* o_e, oa, *or* ow.

A. Read and copy each list word. Circle the letters that make the long-*o* sound. Watch for a word that has an unexpected silent letter. Then organize the list words by the letters making the long-*o* sound.

List Words

		o_e	ow
1. toad	1. _____	_____	_____
2. grow	2. _____	_____	_____
3. nose	3. _____	_____	_____
4. boat	4. _____		
5. snow	5. _____	*oa*	
6. broke	6. _____	_____	
7. close	7. _____	_____	
8. soap	8. _____	_____	
9. coat	9. _____	_____	
10. know	10. _____		

Challenge Words

11. show	11. _____
12. wrote	12. _____
13. those	13. _____

B. Can you find all ten list words hidden two times? Circle them.

brocoatknsoapow   noknowplbrokese   boclosewtoadoatn

snowabrokeknow   bogrowboatlosen   clonosegrowocoat

closeknosnowese   knonoseowsoape   toadyowboatnown

Use a list word to complete each analogy.

1. *Bathing suit* is to *summer* as _____ is to *winter*.
2. A *train* is to *tracks* as a _____ is to *water*.
3. A *knob* is to *door* as a _____ is to *face*.
4. *See* is to *saw* as *break* is to _____.
5. *Rain* is to *warm* as _____ is to *cold*.
6. A *tiger* is to *mammal* as a _____ is to *amphibian*.
7. *Drink* is to *drank* as _____ is to *knew*.
8. *Shampoo* is to *hair* as _____ is to *body*.

Use the clues to identify the list words. Move the sleds down the hill by circling the answers. The sled that reaches the bottom first is the winner!

9. to get bigger
10. used to smell
11. used to clean
12. knit – it + ow
13. antonym for *open*
14. a type of transportation
15. chow – ch + sn
16. used to keep warm

grow

soap

nose

close

boat

know

coat

snow

Write each challenge word three times.

_____   _____   _____

_____   _____   _____

_____   _____   _____

Scholastic

Some of the common spellings for **long-vowel sounds** are:

a_e	e_e	i_e	o_e
ai, ay	ea, ee	y, igh	oa, ow

A. Read and copy each list word. Circle the letters that make the long vowel sound. Then organize the list words by their long vowel sounds.

 List Words

1. deep
2. hole
3. ride
4. meal
5. snail
6. blow
7. game
8. lay
9. goat
10. might

long-a sound

_____

_____

long-i sound

_____

_____

_____

long-o sound

_____

long-e sound

_____

_____

1. _____
2. _____
3. _____
4. _____
5. _____
6. _____
7. _____
8. _____
9. _____
10. _____

🏆 **Challenge Words**

11. globe
12. became
13. smile

11. _____
12. _____
13. _____

B. Unscramble the letters to spell list words.

1. bowl _____
2. alins _____
3. mega _____
4. alem _____
5. yal _____
6. deir _____
7. tago _____
8. leoh _____
9. githm _____
10. eped _____

Scholastic

Write four sentences using at least two list words.

1. _____

2. _____

3. _____

4. _____

 Crack the code to spell each list word.

1	2	3	4	5	6	7	8	9	10	11	12	13	14	15	16	17
g	a	w	r	s	n	i	l	y	d	p	o	t	b	m	h	e

5. 1–2–15–17

_____

6. 16–12–8–17

_____

7. 8–2–9

_____

8. 15–17–2–8

_____

9. 1–12–2–13

_____

10. 10–17–17–11

_____

11. 15–7–1–16–13

_____

12. 4–7–10–17

_____

13. 14–8–12–3

_____

14. 5–6–2–7–8

_____

 Write the challenge word that belongs in each group.

become, becoming,	map, atlas,	smirk, frown,

Scholastic

The **long-*u* sound** *can be spelled with the letters* oo *or* u_e.

A. Read and copy each list word. Circle the letters that make the long-*u* sound. Watch for a word that has an unexpected spelling. Organize the list words by the letters making the long-*u* sound.

 List Words

		oo	**u_e**
1. room	**1.** _____	_____	_____
2. food	**2.** _____	_____	_____
3. tube	**3.** _____	_____	_____
4. mule	**4.** _____	_____	_____
5. moon	**5.** _____		_____
6. rule	**6.** _____	**unexpected**	
7. spoon	**7.** _____	**spelling**	
8. cute	**8.** _____	_____	
9. tune	**9.** _____		
10. who	**10.** _____		

Challenge Words

11. school   **11.** _____

12. goose   **12.** _____

13. scooter   **13.** _____

B. Change one letter in each word to spell a list word.

1. cube _____ *or* _____   **2.** zoom _____

3. tube _____   **4.** why _____   **5.** role _____

6. spook _____   **7.** noon _____   **8.** fool _____

9. male _____

Scholastic

A. Use a list word to complete each sentence.

1. A _____ is a mammal similar to a donkey.

2. There is a _____ baby mule at the zoo.

3. The baby mule gets anxious when he wants _____.

4. He has plenty of _____ to play in his pen.

5. One zoo _____ is that visitors cannot feed the mule.

6. The _____ revolves around Earth.

7. _____ is going to the football game?

8. My baby sister has learned to eat with a _____.

9. Have you heard this _____ before?

10. I found a _____ of toothpaste in my suitcase.

B. Follow the clues to complete the puzzle.

Across

2. rhymes with *groom*

5. a breakfast utensil

8. the base word of *ruler*

10. a synonym for *song*

Down

1. a question word

3. seen in the night sky

4. bread, fruit, vegetables

6. a stubborn mammal

7. an antonym for *ugly*

9. rhymes with *cube*

Write the challenge word that finishes each analogy.

11. A unicycle has one wheel. A _____ has two wheels.

12. A baby cow is a calf. A baby _____ is a gosling.

13. We play on a playground. We learn in a _____.

Scholastic

When the **long-***u* **sound** *is found at the end of a word, it can be spelled with the letters* ew *or* ue.

A. Read each list word. Circle the letters that make the long-*u* sound. Watch for a word that has an unexpected spelling. Then organize the list words by the letters making the long-*u* sound.

List Words   *ew*   *ue*

1. few   1. _____   _____   _____

2. new   2. _____   _____   _____

3. true   3. _____   _____   _____

4. blue   4. _____   _____   _____

5. grew   5. _____   _____

6. flew   6. _____   _____   **unexpected spelling**

7. glue   7. _____

8. drew   8. _____   _____

9. threw   9. _____

10. two   10. _____

Challenge Words

11. due   11. _____

12. dew   12. _____

13. knew   13. _____

B. Change the first and last letters of each word to spell a list word.

1. grub _____   2. owl _____   3. let _____ *and* _____

4. sled _____   5. club _____ *and* _____

Circle ten misspelled words. Write them correctly on the lines.

A True Blue Friend

"Today was a great day at school," Mark said as he thrue the door open. He sat down at the table and took a fue grapes from the bowl. "We drooe pictures to show the parts of a plant. Before I could glew my pictures in place, Drew walked by and brushed them onto the floor. I was so mad! I had to draw tow noow pictures! Then something pretty cool happened. Matthew came over and helped me. We flewe through the work together. I grue less angry then."

Mark's mom replied, "Matthew really is a troo blewe friend."

1. _____ 2. _____ 3. _____ 4. _____ 5. _____

6. _____ 7. _____ 8. _____ 9. _____ 10. _____

 Use addition and subtraction to spell each list word.

11. flag − ag + ew = _____   **12.** glad − ad + ue = _____

13. net − t + w = _____   **14.** toe − oe + wo = _____

15. drum − um + ew = _____   **16.** grip − ip + ew = _____

17. trap − ap + ue = _____   **18.** fur − ur + ew = _____

19. crew − c + th = _____   **20.** blob − ob + ue = _____

 Write the challenge word that matches the definition.

21. drops of water sometimes found on grass early in the morning _____

22. something owed or expected to arrive _____

23. the past tense of *know* _____

Scholastic

➡ *The letters* u, oo, *and* ou *can all sound like* oo *in* **good**.

A. Read and copy each list word. Circle the letters that make the short *oo* sound. Watch for three words that have unexpected spellings. Then organize the list words by the letters that make the short *oo* sound.

List Words

u

1. good   1. _____   _____
2. book   2. _____   _____
3. put   3. _____   _____
4. could   4. _____
5. look   5. _____   *oo*
6. pull   6. _____   _____
7. would   7. _____   _____
8. push   8. _____   _____
9. foot   9. _____   _____
10. should   10. _____

🏆 **Challenge Words**

11. stood   11. _____
12. shook   12. _____
13. cookbook   13. _____

B. 👀 Circle the word that is spelled correctly.

1. shood	should	2. louk	look	3. put	poot		
4. foot	fout	5. cood	could	6. gude	good		
7. pul	pull	8. book	booke	9. woud	would		
10. puch	push							

Scholastic

Write the list word that matches each clue.

1. I am the antonym for *push*. I am _____.

2. When I am plural, I become *feet*. I am _____.

3. I have a homonym that is spelled *wood*. I am _____.

4. Use your eyes to do this. I am _____.

5. I am a synonym for *shove*. I am _____.

6. I am a noun. I am made of paper. I am a _____.

7. I am a three-letter word. I am _____.

8. I am less than *great*. I am _____.

9. We rhyme with *good*. We are _____, _____, and _____.

Circle each list word hidden in the puzzle. The words go across, down, or diagonally.

g	p	u	s	h	k	w	p	u	t	f
b	p	u	o	h	s	b	l	c	j	o
o	h	c	l	n	o	i	r	o	t	o
o	l	q	v	l	d	u	b	u	o	t
k	w	o	u	l	d	c	l	l	a	k
f	m	e	d	s	g	o	o	d	t	l

 Write the challenge word that finishes each exclamation.

10. We _____ on the back of a dolphin!

11. The earthquake _____ the house!

12. This is a great _____!

In some words, two letters work together to make one sound. The two letters are called a **digraph**.

A. Read and copy each list word. Circle the letters that make one new sound. Then organize the list words by the letters that make the new sound.

List Words

1. wish
2. chase
3. shell
4. shut
5. than
6. chat
7. white
8. them
9. which
10. what

sh

1. _____
2. _____
3. _____
4. _____
5. _____
6. _____
7. _____
8. _____
9. _____
10. _____

sh
_____
_____
_____

wh
_____
_____

wh and ch
_____

ch
_____
_____

th
_____
_____

Challenge Words

11. there
12. where
13. these

11. _____
12. _____
13. _____

B. Can you find all ten list words hidden two times? Circle them.

awshellchwisht   thchasethemack   whshutshchatn

whichthannth   shwhiteafwhatin   chasetwhatente

shutthanewish   prshellenchathir   whichwhitethem

Scholastic

📖 Use a list word to complete each analogy.

1. To trot is to run. To _____ is to talk.

2. Grass is green. Snow is _____.

3. *Him* means one person. _____ means more than one person.

4. A rock is found in the dirt. A _____ is found in the ocean.

5. *High* is the antonym for *low*. _____ is the antonym for *open*.

6. *See* is a homonym for *sea*. _____ is a homonym for *witch*.

7. *Chair* rhymes with *hair*. *Pan* rhymes with _____.

8. To run fast is to scurry. To run after is to _____.

9. Make a play in a game. Make a _____ on a star.

10. *Hat* rhymes with *that*. *Hut* rhymes with _____ and _____.

😊 Complete each puzzle with two list words.

11. [puzzle with letters u, n]

12. w, e, t

13. a, e

14. t

15. c

⭐ Write each challenge word three times.

_____ _____ _____

_____ _____ _____

_____ _____ _____

*In some words two letters work together to make one sound. The **long-u sound** can be spelled with the letters* oo, u_e, ew, *and* ue. *The **short-oo sound** can be spelled with the letters* u, oo, *and* ou.

A. Read and copy each list word. Watch for a word that has an unexpected spelling. Then organize the list words by the listed sounds.

List Words

		long-*u* sound as in *room*	*ch, th, wh,* or *sh*
1. bush	1. _____		
2. tool	2. _____	_____	_____
3. thin	3. _____	_____	_____
4. blew	4. _____	_____	_____
5. chest	5. _____		_____
6. took	6. _____	short-*oo* sound as in *good*	_____
7. brush	7. _____		
8. shape	8. _____	_____	
9. clue	9. _____	_____	
10. whale	10. _____		

Challenge Words

11. balloon	11. _____
12. choose	12. _____
13. shoe	13. _____

B. Unscramble the letters to spell list words.

1. alhew _____   2. sbuhr _____   3. shetc _____

4. olot _____   5. phesa _____   6. eluc _____

7. elwb _____   8. niht _____   9. shub _____

10. okot _____

Scholastic

A. Write four sentences using at least two list words in each.

1. _____

2. _____

3. _____

4. _____

B. Riddle time! Use the clues to write each list word in the boxes. When you have finished, the shaded boxes will spell the answer to the riddle.

What has ten letters and starts with gas?

1. A square is a _____.
2. rhymes with *blue*
3. a part of the body
4. past tense of *take*
5. a hammer
6. a plant
7. antonym for *thick*
8. an ocean animal
9. homonym for *blue*

Write the challenge word that belongs in each group.

sock, boot,	decide, pick,	circus, clown,

The sound a vowel makes often changes when it is followed by an r.

A. Read and copy each list word. Circle the "vowel plus *r*" spellings. Watch for words that have unexpected spellings. Then organize the list words by the number of letters they have.

List Words

three letters   **five letters**

1. smart   1. _____   _____   _____
2. her   2. _____   _____
3. bird   3. _____   **four letters** _____
4. more   4. _____   _____
5. curl   5. _____   _____
6. sharp   6. _____   _____
7. were   7. _____   _____
8. first   8. _____   _____
9. hurt   9. _____   _____
10. your   10. _____

Challenge Words

11. morning   11. _____
12. third   12. _____
13. before   13. _____

B. Write a list word that begins with the same sound as the picture.

1. _____   2. _____   *and*   _____

3. _____   4. _____   5.  _____

6. _____   7. _____   8. _____

Scholastic

Circle ten misspelled words. Write them correctly on the lines.

Kia was given a berd for her eighth birthday. She named her Sweetie. It was the forst pet Kia had ever had. Sometimes Kia's bird would sit on hir shoulder. "Yor bird is really smurt," everyone told Kia. One day Kia and Sweetie wer sitting on the front porch. A wild bird with a cirl on its head landed nearby. Sweetie flew from Kia's shoulder and onto a branch near the wild bird. The wild bird flew away. Kia waited for Sweetie to fly back, but her bird didn't. Sweetie seemed to be hert. Kia lifted Sweetie down and noticed how sharpe the branch was. Kia said, "You can't fly with the wild birds. They have mor experience than you do, Sweetie." The bird seemed to understand and climbed back onto Kia's shoulder.

1. _____   2. _____   3. _____   4. _____

5. _____   6. _____   7. _____   8. _____

9. _____   10. _____

 Follow the clues to play tic-tac-toe. As you find each answer, mark an *X* or *O*. Do you get three in a row?

11. I am the antonym for *dull*. Mark an *O*.

12. I begin like the word *birthday*. Mark an *X*.

13. I come before *second*. Mark an *O*.

14. I am the antonym for *less*. Mark an *X*.

15. I show that a girl owns something. Mark an *O*.

16. I am a synonym for *intelligent*. Mark an *X*.

17. I rhyme with *shirt*. Mark an *O*.

18. I rhyme with *her*. Mark an *X*.

19. I describe a pig's tail. Mark an *O*.

her	were	hurt
bird	curl	smart
first	more	sharp

Draw a picture to illustrate each challenge word. Label the picture.

Two vowels that come together and make one new sound are called a **diphthong**. *In some words, vowel combinations come together to make a completely new sound. The letters* ou *and* ow *often make the same sound. For example:* **out** *and* **cow**

A. Read and copy each list word. Circle the *ou* or *ow* spelling. Then organize the list words by either *ou* or *ow*.

List Words

		ou	ow
1. how	1. _____	_____	_____
2. clown	2. _____	_____	_____
3. house	3. _____	_____	_____
4. down	4. _____	_____	_____
5. now	5. _____	_____	_____
6. shout	6. _____		
7. about	7. _____		
8. town	8. _____		
9. count	9. _____		
10. our	10. _____		

Challenge Words

11. found	11. _____
12. crown	12. _____
13. mouth	13. _____

B. Change the last two letters in each word to spell a list word.

1. shore _____

2. abode _____

3. his _____

4. couch _____

5. torn _____

6. hound _____

7. net _____

8. cloud _____

9. oat _____

10. door _____

Scholastic

Complete the story using each of the list words.

The circus has come to _____! My favorite part is watching the _____ shoot out of the cannon. We all _____ from 10 _____ to zero and then yell, "Blast off!" Then we cover _____ ears because the cannon is loud. You can hear the clown _____ "Wheee," as he flies over our heads. He flies for _____ two minutes. Then he disappears. "Where is he _____?" everyone asks. Suddenly, the clown jumps out of a dog's _____. "Wow! _____ did he do that?" we all wonder.

Use the clues to identify the list words. Move the clowns along the path by circling the answers. The clown that reaches the circus tent first is the winner.

1. the antonym for *up*
2. Where is ____ dog?
3. a circus performer
4. at this time
5. a synonym for *home*
6. smaller than a city
7. 1, 2, 3 . . .
8. a question word
9. not exact
10. a synonym for *yell*

down   house   town
our
clown   now
count
how
shout
about

Write the challenge word that finishes each question.

11. Has he _____ his notebook yet?

12. Can you talk with your _____ closed?

13. Did you notice all of the jewels in the ancient _____?

The letters oi *and* oy *often make the same sound. For example:* oil *and* boy

A. Read and copy each list word. Circle the *oi* or *oy* spelling. Then organize the list words by either *oi* or *oy*.

List Words

		oi	*oy*
1. oil	**1.** _____	_____	_____
2. boy	**2.** _____	_____	_____
3. toy	**3.** _____	_____	_____
4. join	**4.** _____	_____	_____
5. soil	**5.** _____	_____	
6. joy	**6.** _____	_____	
7. boil	**7.** _____		
8. enjoy	**8.** _____		
9. coin	**9.** _____		
10. point	**10.** _____		

Challenge Words

11. noise	**11.** _____
12. voice	**12.** _____
13. annoy	**13.** _____

B. Circle the word that is spelled correctly.

1. joi	joy	**2.** soyl	soil	**3.** toy	toye		
4. koin	coin	**5.** boy	boiy	**6.** joyn	join		
7. enjoy	injoy	**8.** oil	oyl	**9.** boyl	boil		
10. poynt	point							

Scholastic

Use a list word to complete each analogy.

1. A fish lives in water. A flower lives in _____.

2. *Woman* is to *man* as *girl* is to _____.

3. *Cat* is to *at* as *boil* is to _____.

4. The nose is part of an airplane. The _____ is part of a pencil.

5. Water will freeze when it is cold. Water will _____ when it is hot.

6. *Rough* is the antonym of *smooth*. *Dislike* is the antonym of _____.

7. To separate is to break apart. To _____ is to come together.

8. Sadness is pain. Happiness is _____.

9. A tire is made of rubber. A _____ is made of metal.

10. A dog plays with a bone. A child plays with a _____.

Use the Braille code to spell each list word.

b	c	e	i	j	l	n	o	p	s	t	y
⠃	⠉	⠑	⠊	⠚	⠇	⠝	⠕	⠏	⠎	⠞	⠽

11. ___ ___ ___

12. ___ ___ ___ ___

13. ___ ___ ___ ___

14. ___ ___ ___

15. ___ ___ ___

16. ___ ___ ___ ___

17. ___ ___ ___ ___ ___

18. ___ ___ ___

19. ___ ___ ___ ___ ___

20. ___ ___ ___ ___ ___

Write the challenge word that finishes each analogy.

21. *Scream* is a synonym for *yell*. *Bug* is a synonym for _____.

22. You walk with your feet. You sing with your _____.

23. You hear whispers in the library. You hear _____ on the playground.

The letters aw *make the sound in the word* **law**. *The letters* all *make the sound in the word* **ball**. *These are two different sounds.*

A. Read and copy each list word. Circle the *aw* or *all* spellings. Then organize the list words by either *aw* or *all*.

List Words

List Words		*aw*	*all*
1. tall	**1.** ________	________	________
2. jaw	**2.** ________	________	________
3. ball	**3.** ________	________	________
4. hall	**4.** ________	________	________
5. paw	**5.** ________	________	________
6. saw	**6.** ________		
7. call	**7.** ________		
8. draw	**8.** ________		
9. yawn	**9.** ________		
10. fall	**10.** ________		

Challenge Words

11. dawn **11.** ________

12. claw **12.** ________

13. hawk **13.** ________

B. Write a list word that begins with the same letter as the picture.

1.  ________ **2.**  ________ **3.**  ________

4.  ________ **5.**  ________ **6.**  ________

7.  ________ **8.**  ________ **9.**  ________

Write the list word that matches each clue.

1. I am an animal's foot. I am a _____.

2. You do this when you are sleepy. This is a _____.

3. I am part of your face. I am a _____.

4. I am a season called *autumn*. I am _____.

5. I am an antonym for *short*. I am _____.

6. I am the past tense for *see*. I am _____.

7. I am shaped like a sphere. I am a _____.

8. I am the present tense of *drew*. I am _____.

9. I may be part of your school or house. I am a _____.

10. Your mother may do this at dinnertime. She may _____ you.

 Circle each list word hidden in the puzzle. The words go across, down, or diagonally.

r	h	j	p	d	c	f	a	l	d
b	t	a	y	p	a	w	b	j	r
c	y	b	l	f	l	t	l	a	a
d	a	h	c	l	l	y	a	w	w
k	w	s	a	w	s	f	s	l	l
f	n	e	a	l	l	r	j	p	l

Change the last two letters in each word to spell a challenge word.

11. clip_____

12. hand_____

13. damp_____

Many letters may work together to make a new sound.
Remember these: ar er ir or ur ou ow aw all oi oy

A. Read and copy each list word. Circle the letters that work together.
Then organize the list words by their vowel sounds.

List Words

1. art
2. straw
3. girl
4. south
5. small
6. horse
7. frown
8. sister
9. turn
10. foil

1. _____
2. _____
3. _____
4. _____
5. _____
6. _____
7. _____
8. _____
9. _____
10. _____

words with vowel + r

_____
_____
_____
_____
_____

words with all or aw

_____
_____

word with oi

_____

words with ou or ow

_____
_____

Challenge Words

11. purple
12. round
13. shirt

11. _____
12. _____
13. _____

B. Unscramble the letters to spell list words.

1. rat_____
2. ilof_____
3. stohu_____
4. nutr_____
5. mlsla_____
6. ritses_____
7. norwf_____
8. resoh_____
9. wasrt_____
10. ligr_____

A. Write four sentences using at least two list words in each.

1. _____

2. _____

3. _____

4. _____

B. Riddle time! Use the clues to write each list word in the boxes. When you have finished, the shaded boxes will spell the answer to the riddle.

What do you call a crazy spaceman?

1. helps you take a drink
2. change directions
3. antonym for *big*
4. an animal
5. a class at school
6. antonym for *boy*
7. wrap food in this
8. rhymes with *clown*
9. a direction
10. a girl in your family

Write the challenge word that belongs in each group.

yellow, blue,	square, rectangular,	shoes, pants,

Throughout the year, see if you can learn all the words on this Grade 2 spelling list.

about	clap	foot	light	pick	slide	tool
after	close	fox	lock	point	slip	town
art	clown	from	look	pull	small	toy
ask	clue	frown	made	push	smart	trade
away	coat	game	map	put	snail	trail
ball	coin	girl	mask	read	snake	train
bed	come	glue	meal	ride	snow	true
beg	could	goat	mean	right	soap	try
begged	count	good	meet	room	sock	tub
bend	cry	grew	met	rub	soil	tube
best	curl	grow	might	rule	some	tune
bird	cute	hall	milk	run	south	turn
black	deep	has	miss	running	spoon	two
blew	dot	have	mix	sack	spot	was
blow	down	her	moon	said	stop	went
blue	draw	here	mop	saw	straw	were
boat	drew	hid	more	say	tall	whale
boil	drop	hole	mule	seen	tap	what
book	dropped	horse	must	send	tapping	wheel
box	dump	house	nest	shape	team	which
boy	dust	how	new	sharp	tent	white
brake	each	hurt	night	shell	than	who
broke	enjoy	jaw	nose	should	them	why
brush	eve	join	now	shout	they	wide
bump	fall	joy	odd	shut	thin	wish
bush	few	kick	off	sister	threw	with
call	first	kiss	oil	skip	time	would
chase	flew	know	our	skipping	tip	yawn
chat	foil	last	pain	sky	toad	yet
chest	food	lay	paw	sleep	took	your

Scholastic

Phonics/Spelling Practice Test

Fill in the bubble next to the correct answer.

1. Which word rhymes with *shake*?

   ○ **A**   seed

   ○ **B**   date

   ○ **C**   bake

   ○ **D**   skate

2. Which word rhymes with *seed*?

   ○ **F**   fear

   ○ **G**   ate

   ○ **H**   weed

   ○ **J**   wait

3. Which word has the short-*a* sound?

   ○ **A**   bait

   ○ **B**   clap

   ○ **C**   made

   ○ **D**   bay

Phonics/Spelling Practice Test

Fill in the bubble next to the correct answer.

4. Which word has the long-*e* sound?

   ○ **A**   bench

   ○ **B**   next

   ○ **C**   met

   ○ **D**   feed

5. Which word does NOT have the short-*o* sound?

   ○ **F**   clock

   ○ **G**   mop

   ○ **H**   boat

   ○ **J**   stop

6. Which word rhymes with tub?

   ○ **A**   was

   ○ **B**   dump

   ○ **C**   dust

   ○ **D**   rub

Phonics/Spelling Practice Test

Fill in the bubble next to the correct answer.

7. Which is the correct spelling of the past tense of clap?

○ **A** clapping

○ **B** claped

○ **C** clapped

○ **D** clapt

8. Which is the correct spelling of the past tense of drop?

○ **F** dropt

○ **G** droped

○ **H** dropping

○ **J** dropped

9. Which word does NOT have the long-*a* sound?

○ **A** have

○ **B** hay

○ **C** snail

○ **D** made

Scholastic

Phonics/Spelling Practice Test

Fill in the bubble next to the correct answer.

10. Which answer solves the problem below?

crew – c + th =

- ◯ **A** threw
- ◯ **B** creth
- ◯ **C** thcrew
- ◯ **D** weth

11. Which word is spelled correctly?

- ◯ **F** shood
- ◯ **G** brooke
- ◯ **H** should
- ◯ **J** woud

12. Which word is spelled correctly?

- ◯ **A** puch
- ◯ **B** push
- ◯ **C** coud
- ◯ **D** louk

Scholastic

Vocabulary

Words! Words! Words! As children learn new words they learn that words can do many things. They can tell direction (above/below). They may tell opposites (up/down). They may name things (elephant/brother). And they can describe things (long, beautiful, silly).

The activities in this section introduce commonly used words that will become part of your child's everyday vocabulary. Children who know lots of words become strong readers.

What to Do
Have your child complete the activity pages. Then cut out the Vocabulary Flash Cards on pages 121–125. Review them throughout the year with your child. Have your child add new words he or she learns at home and in school.

Keep On Going!
Have your child find antonyms or synonyms of the words on the flash cards. Also encourage your child to use the word cards to build sentences.

antonym

Synonym

Look at the picture. Circle the word in each row of words that names or describes the picture.

1. carrot   apple   pencil
2. black   orange   green
3. food   far   car

1. mop   broom   book
2. drive   sweet   sweep
3. clear   clean   clap

1. tree   flowers   flow
2. leaf   leaves   leap
3. smile   smack   smart

1. ducks   doors   cluck
2. two   three   four
3. quack   quick   quiet

Scholastic

Look at the picture. Circle the word in each row of words that names or describes the picture.

1. legs eggs ever

2. sack crow cracks

3. three six nine

1. fish wish find

2. boat bowl bow

3. just run jump

1. candle cake can

2. flame far flip

3. milk map melt

1. bat boy bee

2. dream drink drive

3. woods wave walk

Scholastic

Look at the picture. Circle the word in each row of words that names or describes the picture.

1. horse   goat   zebra

2. stripes   sticks   stones

3. after   animal   ant

1. frog   fruit   from

2. torn   top   tongue

3. flip   flap   fly

1. green   gone   ghost

2. with   white   while

3. boo   broom   box

1. tree   turtle   twist

2. shed   ship   shell

3. sit   stop   star

Scholastic

Antonyms *are words with opposite meanings.*

Write an antonym for each clue
to complete the crossword puzzle.
Use the words in the Word Bank
below to help you.

Across	**Down**
1. smile	**2.** new
4. right	**3.** south
6. clean	**4.** big
9. sad	**5.** last
11. start	**7.** close
12. wide	**8.** lost
14. rough	**10.** down
16. under	**13.** forget
	15. short

Word Bank

tall	over	smooth
left	dirty	across
first	north	happy
old	open	remember
stop	frown	narrow
little	found	

Scholastic

Read each sentence. Circle the word that means the opposite of the underlined word.

1. You must <u>push</u> the door to close it.

pull   hit   brake

2. <u>Nothing</u> was in the mailbox today.

fun   everything   stop

3. My glass was <u>full</u>.

clear   red   empty

4. I saw a pretty bird <u>outside</u>.

away   home   inside

5. Susan is always the <u>first</u> person in line.

second   smartest   last

6. After we <u>work</u>, we will read a book.

play   study   eat

7. The movie last night made me <u>laugh</u>.

sick   happy   cry

8. We must be <u>quiet</u> in the library.

noisy   awake   safe

Read each sentence. Circle the word that means the opposite of the underlined word.

1. We found some <u>large</u> starfish at the beach.

      blue   small   dirty

2. Please do not run <u>inside</u>.

      outside   around   after

3. My friends and I are always <u>together</u>.

      busy   apart   quietly

4. You can <u>stay</u> if you want to.

      talk   rest   leave

5. Do not <u>sit</u> while he is speaking.

      talk   stand   cry

6. My grades are getting <u>better</u>.

      higher   worse   as good as

7. This is a very <u>dark</u> room.

      light   funny   old

8. <u>None</u> of the students went to the play.

      Some   Two   All

A **synonym** *is a word that means the same or nearly the same as another word.*

Circle every other letter. Write the circled letters in order on the line to name the synonym for each word. The first one has been done for you.

begin	s Ⓢ y Ⓣ n Ⓐ o Ⓡ n Ⓣ	**start**
glad	y h m a s p a p r y	_____
tell	e s w a o y	_____
loud	r n d o s i t s h y	_____
little	a s t m h a a l v l	_____
look	e p t e h e e k	_____
large	s b a i m g	_____
fearful	e a m f e r a a n i i d	_____
group	n s g e s t	_____

Write the letters you did not circle in order on the blanks to complete the sentence.

_ _ _ _ _ _ _ _   _ _ _   _ _ _ _ _ _   _ _ _ _

_ _ _ _   _ _ _   _ _ _ _ _ _   _ _ _ _ _ _ _ _ .

Scholastic

Read each sentence. Circle the word that means almost the same as the underlined word.

1. Tom was outside for <u>just</u> five minutes.

    after   only   over

2. Please <u>save</u> this seat for me.

    bring   buy   keep

3. The three bears lived in the <u>woods</u>.

    forest   house   tent

4. Pam went to bed because she was <u>sleepy</u>.

    quiet   tired   awake

5. I am <u>glad</u> to see that you have done your work.

    angry   asking   happy

6. First the cat <u>sniffed</u> the food, then she ate it.

    smelled   pulled   pushed

7. Mary <u>tore</u> her best dress.

    mended   ripped   broke

8. The teacher <u>spoke</u> in a soft voice.

    cheered   screamed   talked

Scholastic

Homonyms *are words that have more than one meaning.*

Write the word from a star that can be used in both blanks in each sentence. The first one has been done for you.

quarter   rest   train   star

down   jam   kind   yard

1. The _____ star _____ of the team won the medal with a gold _____ star _____.

2. It was a _____ to five when I spent my last _____.

3. We found a _____ of ribbon while playing in the _____.

4. Juan threw the _____ pillow _____ from the top bunk.

5. Amber wanted to _____ before finishing the _____ of her homework.

6. The _____ woman let me choose my favorite _____ of ice cream.

7. Christy needs to _____ her dog before they ride on the _____.

8. Scott ate toast and _____ during the traffic _____.

Scholastic

Homophones *are words that sound alike but have different spellings and different meanings.*

Add or subtract letters to spell the homophone of the first word. Write the homophone that fits the sentence. The first one has been done for you.

1. deer – er + ar = __dear__   The __deer__ jumped the fence to safety.

2. two – w = _____   A duet is made of _____ singers.

3. sun – u + o = _____   The father took his _____ to the game.

4. scent – s = _____   The _____ of flowers filled the room.

5. chili – i + ly = _____   Wear a coat when it is _____.

6. their – ir + re = _____   Your books are _____ on the table.

7. know – k – w = _____   The sign says _____ swimming.

8. hair – ir + re = _____   Brush your _____ before school.

9. wee – e = _____   He was a _____ little lad.

10. here – re + ar = _____   Listen closely to _____ the directions.

11. weight – eight + ait = _____   The rock's _____ was great.

12. break – eak + ake = _____   It is time for a _____.

Scholastic

A **compound word** *is a word made by joining two words together to make a new word.*

Complete the crossword puzzle with the missing part of each compound word. Use the Word Bank to help you.

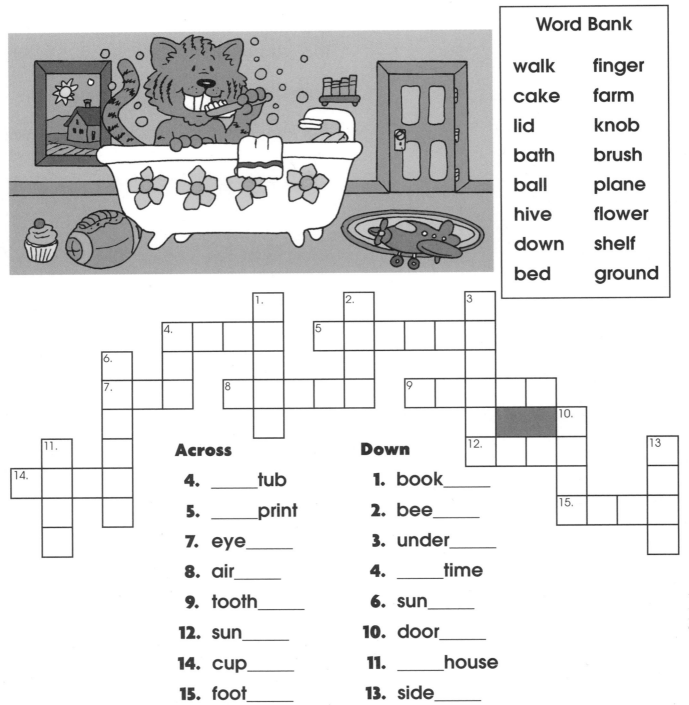

Word Bank

walk	finger
cake	farm
lid	knob
bath	brush
ball	plane
hive	flower
down	shelf
bed	ground

Across

4. _____tub
5. _____print
7. eye_____
8. air_____
9. tooth_____
12. sun_____
14. cup_____
15. foot_____

Down

1. book_____
2. bee_____
3. under_____
4. _____time
6. sun_____
10. door_____
11. _____house
13. side_____

Scholastic

Circle the words from the word list in the puzzle below. The words go across and down.

READING WORD LIST

read   bookstore
book   words
cover   pictures
pages   spine
library   fun

r e a d n b c v w s x c
f m p a g e s d o p a o
u f g h k j p l r i o v
n b n c m v b n d n m e
q e r b o o k o s e p r
b o o k s t o r e c v b
b q e p i c t u r e s h
l i b r a r y a u f g d

Circle the words from the word list in the puzzle below. The words go across and down.

WATER FRIENDS WORD LIST

WHALE	SHARK
FISH	EEL
CLAM	SHRIMP
LOBSTER	TURTLE
DOLPHIN	SEAHORSE

```
W H A L E E T S Z C T F
L A S E P E Y H B X U I
O F D P R L V A N M R S
B G H O J K L R E K T H
S O C L A M I K U Y L T
T A S D O L P H I N E D
E S E A H O R S E G H F
R R D G J S H R I M P T
```

Scholastic

Circle the words from the word list in the puzzle below. The words go across and down.

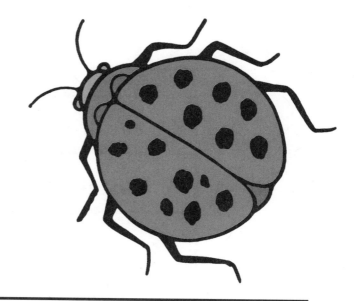

```
INSECTS WORD LIST

   bee          roach
mosquito      beetle
   ant        ladybug
grasshopper     moth
  cricket     butterfly
```

```
g r a s s h o p p e r c
b w e r l a d y b u g r
e y b u t t e r f l y i
e u i k m n a n t b f c
m o t h l j k u y s a k
r t e q a r o a c h o e
b e e t l e y s i m p t
n f h j m o s q u i t o
```

Scholastic

Unscramble each geometry word and write it on the line. Use the words in the box to help you. Then color the box and the matching shape in the color listed below the line.

circle	rectangle	cylinder	cube	oval
square	triangle	cone	diamond	hexagon

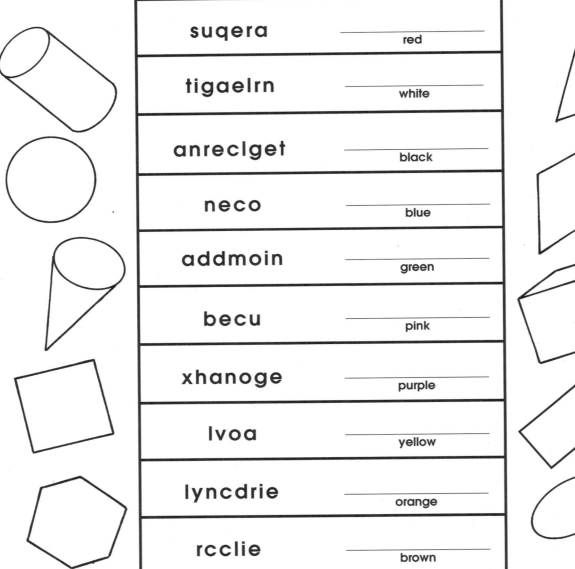

suqera _____ red

tigaelrn _____ white

anreclget _____ black

neco _____ blue

addmoin _____ green

becu _____ pink

xhanoge _____ purple

lvoa _____ yellow

lyncdrie _____ orange

rcclie _____ brown

Scholastic

Use the chart to write the missing words.

g	h	v	y	l	n	q	o	e	i	c	t	m	f	u	r	b	s	d	a	w
1	2	3	4	5	6	7	8	9	10	11	12	13	14	15	16	17	18	19	20	21

1. When you ___ ___ ___ numbers, the answer is the ___ ___ ___.
              20 19 19   18 15 13

2. When you ___ ___ ___ ___ ___ ___ ___ ___ numbers, the answer
                  18 15 17 12 16 20 11 12

is the ___ ___ ___ ___ ___ ___ ___ ___ ___ ___.
       19 10 14 14 9 16 9 6 11 9

3. The words ___ ___ ___ ___ ___ ___ ___ ___ ___ ___ and
            20 5 12 8 1 9 12 2 9 16

___ ___ ___ ___ ___ in a word problem tell you to add.
12 8 12 20 5

4. The words ___ ___ ___ ___   ___ ___ ___ ___ and
            2 20 3 9   5 9 14 12

___ ___ ___   ___ ___ ___ ___   ___ ___ ___ ___ in a word
2 8 21   13 20 6 4   13 8 16 9

problem tell you to subtract.

5. Two numbers of the same value are ___ ___ ___ ___ ___.
                                   9 7 15 20 5

6. When you ___ ___ ___ ___ ___ a problem, you get the answer.
            18 8 5 3 9

Use the words in the box to label each part of the flower and to complete the sentences below.

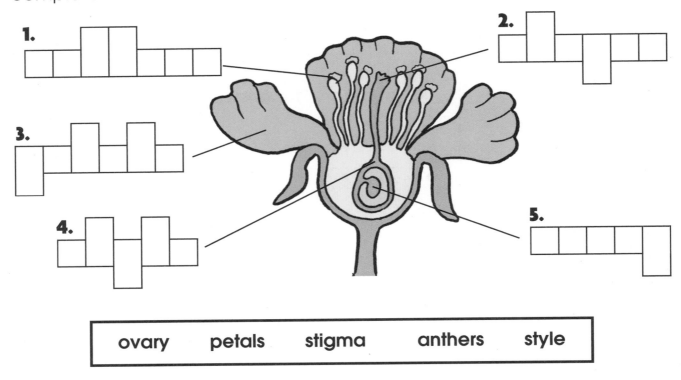

1.

2.

3.

4.

5.

| ovary | petals | stigma | anthers | style |

A flower is important in the life cycle of a plant because it contains the parts for reproduction. The colorful **6.** __ __ t __ __ __ and sepals protect the flower when it is in bud. The sticky part in the middle of the flower is the **7.** __ __ __ g __ __ . Around the stigma are **8.** __ n __ __ __ __ __ which are tiny stems with knobs on top. Inside the anthers is a golden dust called pollen. In the base of the flower is the **9.** __ v __ __ __ . Growing out of the ovary is the **10.** __ __ y __ __ . When ripe, the anthers burst open sending out clouds of pollen. The pollen is carried to the stigma of another flower. This is called pollination.

A. Use the words in the box to label each part of an insect and to complete the sentences below.

1._____

2._____

3._____

4._____

5._____

6._____

7._____

8._____

B.

An insect's $\underset{3}{\rule{1.5cm}{0.4pt}}$ includes the $\underset{9}{\rule{1.5cm}{0.4pt}}$ and

$\underset{10}{\rule{0.5cm}{0.4pt}} \underset{2}{\rule{1.5cm}{0.4pt}}$. Three pairs of $\underset{6}{\rule{1.5cm}{0.4pt}}$ are

connected to the $\underset{8}{\rule{0.5cm}{0.4pt}} \underset{1}{\rule{1.5cm}{0.4pt}}$. Most insects

have one or two pair of _____. The tip of the

$\underset{7}{\rule{0.5cm}{0.4pt}} \underset{4}{\rule{1.5cm}{0.4pt}}$ may have a tube for laying eggs

or a $\underset{5}{\rule{2cm}{0.4pt}}$.

stinger
wings
head
antennae
thorax
eyes
legs
abdomen

C. Use the number code above to learn some interesting facts about insects.

There are more than $\underset{1 \ 2 \ 3}{\rule{2cm}{0.4pt}} \underset{4 \ 5 \ 6 \ 6 \ 5 \ 1 \ 2}{\rule{3cm}{0.4pt}}$ kinds of insects.

The Goliath $\underset{7 \ 3 \ 3 \ 8 \ 6 \ 3}{\rule{3cm}{0.4pt}}$ grows to more than four inches long.

An $\underset{10 \ 8 \ 6 \ 10 \ 9}{\rule{2.5cm}{0.4pt}}$ moth is about 1,000 times larger than a tiny fairy fly.

Scholastic

Use the code to complete the sentences below. Then write the number of each place in the correct circle on the map.

e	o	f	a	n	s	u	r	l	m	d	h	c	t	p	i	g
1	2	3	4	5	6	7	8	9	10	11	12	13	14	15	16	17

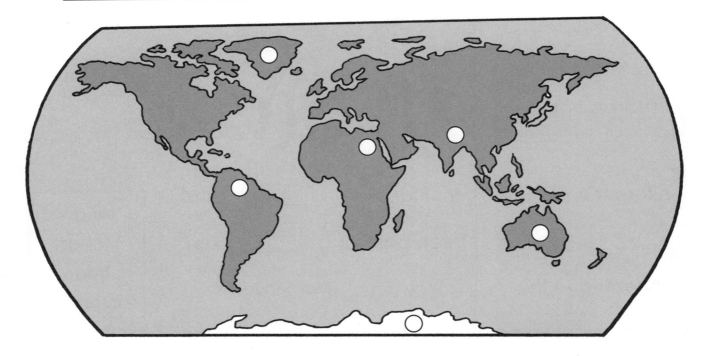

1. The smallest continent on Earth is ___ ___ ___ ___ ___ ___ ___ ___ ___.
　　4　7　6　14　8　4　9　16　4

2. The highest mountain on Earth is Mt. Everest in ___ ___ ___ ___.
　　4　6　16　4

3. The largest island on Earth is ___ ___ ___ ___ ___ ___ ___ ___ ___.
　　17　8　1　1　5　9　4　5　11

4. The longest river on Earth is the Nile on the continent of ___ ___ ___ ___ ___ ___.
　　4　3　8　16　13　4

5. The highest waterfall on Earth is in ___ ___ ___ ___ ___ ___ ___ ___ ___ ___ ___.
　　6　2　7　14　12　　4　10　1　8　16　13　4

6. The coldest place on Earth is ___ ___ ___ ___ ___ ___ ___ ___ ___ ___.
　　4　5　14　4　8　13　14　16　13　4

Scholastic

Write the character trait described in each sentence. Use the words on the caps as clues. Then use the number code to complete the sentence below.

1.

I finished my homework before going out to play.

__ __ __ __ __ __ __ __ __ __ __ __ __ __
4   7

2.

I accidentally took my friend's dollar, but I gave it back.

__ __ __ __ __ __ __
2

3.

I worked with all my neighbors and cleaned the street.

__ __ __ __ __ __ __ __ __ __ __
9 3

4.

I asked the new boy to play with me at recess.

__ __ __ __ __ __ __ __ __ __ __ __ __
6   5

5.

At lunchtime I was very hungry, but I waited my turn in line.

__ __ __ __ __ __ __ __
8   1

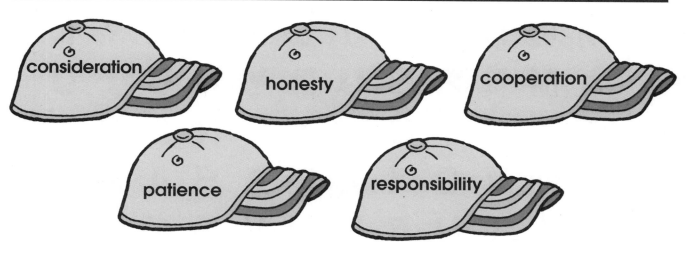

consideration   honesty   cooperation

patience   responsibility

Your __ __ __ __ __ __ __ __ __ is who you are when no one is looking.
        1 2 3 4 5 6 7 8 9

Scholastic

Circle the words from the word list in the puzzle below. The words go across and down.

PLANETS WORD LIST

EARTH	MARS
PLUTO	VENUS
SATURN	NEPTUNE
URANUS	MERCURY
JUPITER	

```
E A R T H K L Q N U W E
F R F G H J Q F E R N R
J U P I T E R K P A O P
M R S E W J L P T N Y L
A M E R C U R Y U U T U
R T D Y G U I O N S R T
S M V C X Z K A E A P O
S A T U R N M V E N U S
```

Scholastic

Circle the words from the word list in the puzzle below. The words go across and down.

SPACE WORD LIST

planets	rocket
solar system	astronaut
moon	comet
stars	meteor
sun	galaxy

```
s o l a r s y s t e m p
m m e t e o r j c k l l
o m o r t i l k o g m a
o s q w e r t k m y b n
n v s t a r s j e s n e
r o c k e t g h t u b t
a s t r o n a u t n v s
g a l a x y f d s a c x
```

Circle the words from the word list in the puzzle below. The words go across and down.

CAREERS WORD LIST

CHEF	FIREFIGHTER
TEACHER	BAKER
FARMER	DOCTOR
PILOT	LAWYER
CAPTAIN	DENTIST

```
F I R E F I G H T E R D
A S D R E P W C Q T F O
B A K E R I M A L E A C
X C V B N L P P K A R T
C H E F O O I T J C M O
E R T Y U T Z A H H E R
D E N T I S T I G E R D
L A W Y E R J N F R A S
```

Scholastic

Circle the words from the word list in the puzzle below. The words go across and down.

MATH WORD LIST

add	borrow
subtract	regroup
plus	sum
minus	difference
equals	math

```
d i f f e r e n c e s q
p w e r e g r o u p u b
l r t y u i o p l k b o
u z a d d f s g h j t r
s x c v n a s u m l r r
w b g e q u a l s u a o
a q m i n u s o h j c w
m a t h i f n d s v t m
```

Scholastic

An **analogy** *is a comparison of two sets of similar objects.*

Complete each analogy with a word on an apple.
Color the apples you used red.

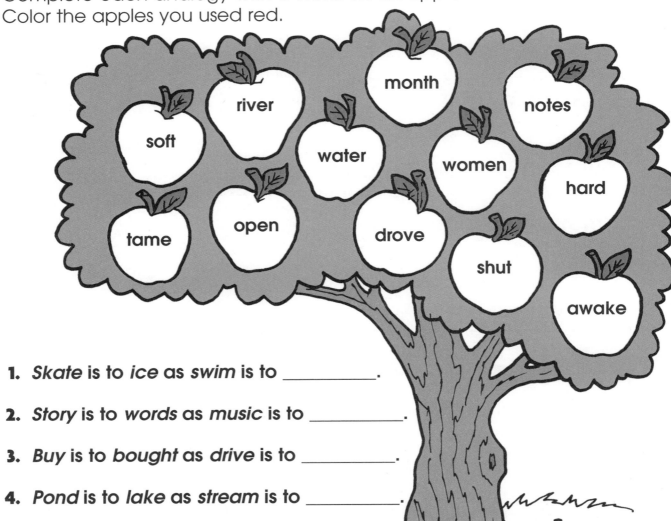

1. *Skate* is to *ice* as *swim* is to _____.

2. *Story* is to *words* as *music* is to _____.

3. *Buy* is to *bought* as *drive* is to _____.

4. *Pond* is to *lake* as *stream* is to _____.

5. *Top* is to *bottom* as *wild* is to _____.

6. *Week* is to *day* as *year* is to _____.

7. *Fast* is to *slow* as *asleep* is to _____.

8. *Man* is to *men* as *woman* is to _____.

Use the apples you did not color to make an analogy.

_____ is to _____ as _____ is to _____.

Scholastic

Complete the analogy on each bat. Use the words on the caps to help you.

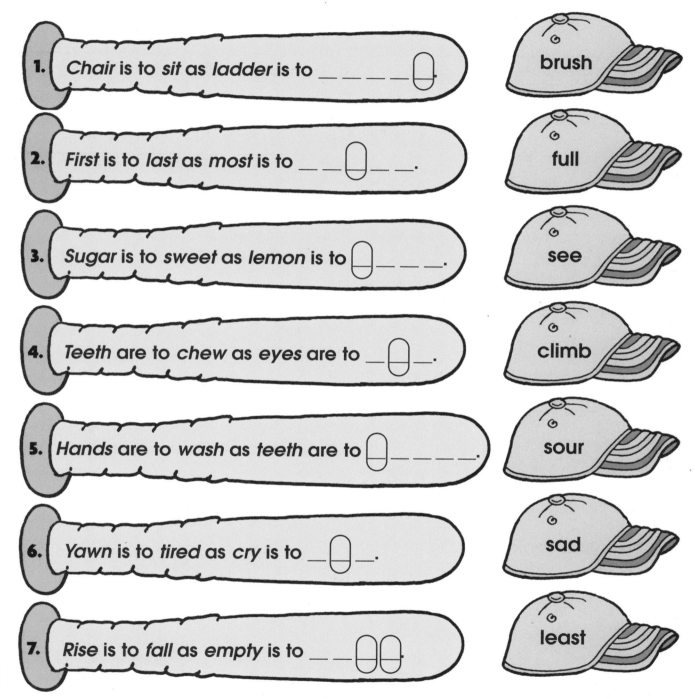

1. Chair is to sit as ladder is to _ _ _ _ _ O .

brush

2. First is to last as most is to _ _ _ O _ _ .

full

3. Sugar is to sweet as lemon is to O _ _ _ _ .

see

4. Teeth are to chew as eyes are to _ O _ .

climb

5. Hands are to wash as teeth are to O _ _ _ _ _ .

sour

6. Yawn is to tired as cry is to _ O _ .

sad

7. Rise is to fall as empty is to _ _ O O _ .

least

Write the circled letters in the blanks in order to find out what sport was first called "rounders." __ __ __ __ __ __ __ __

Scholastic

Read each sentence. Note the underlined words. Complete the second sentence to tell how the words in the first pair and the words in the second pair go together.

> TIP
>
> Stone is to rock as bug is to insect.
> Say to yourself: Stone is another word for rock,
>   and bug is another word for insect.

1. Cap is to lid as spin is to turn.

Cap is another word for lid, and _____ is another word for _____.

2. Shop is to store as stairs are to steps.

Shop is another word for store, and _____ is another word for _____.

3. Boy is to lad as friend is to pal.

Boy is another word for lad, and _____ is another word for _____.

4. Story is to tale as pail is to bucket.

Story is another word for tale, and _____ is another word for _____.

5. Shiver is to shake as mad is to angry.

Shiver is another word for shake, and _____ is another word for _____.

Scholastic

Choose the correct word to complete each sentence.

1. A <u>stick</u> is like a <u>stake</u>, and a <u>cap</u> is like a _____.

   Ⓐ sock   Ⓑ hat   Ⓒ twig

2. A <u>runner</u> is like a <u>racer</u>, and a <u>smile</u> is like a _____.

   Ⓐ frown   Ⓑ face   Ⓒ grin

3. A <u>crowd</u> is like a <u>mob</u>, and a <u>song</u> is like a _____.

   Ⓐ group   Ⓑ tune   Ⓒ flute

4. A <u>dinner</u> is like a <u>supper</u>, and a <u>pot</u> is like a _____.

   Ⓐ pan   Ⓑ cook   Ⓒ meal

5. <u>Fur</u> is like <u>fuzz</u>, and <u>wet</u> is like _____.

   Ⓐ messy   Ⓑ dry   Ⓒ damp

6. <u>Sad</u> is like <u>gloomy</u>, and <u>happy</u> is like _____.

   Ⓐ glad   Ⓑ mad   Ⓒ nice

7. <u>Misty</u> is like <u>foggy</u>, and <u>fast</u> is like _____.

   Ⓐ runner   Ⓑ quick   Ⓒ slow

8. <u>Look</u> is like <u>see</u>, and <u>sleep</u> is like _____.

   Ⓐ nap   Ⓑ wake   Ⓒ find

Scholastic

Choose the correct word to complete each sentence.

1. <u>Rich</u> is the opposite of <u>poor</u>, and <u>weak</u> is the opposite of _____.

    (A) strong   (B) day   (C) frail

2. <u>Give</u> is the opposite of <u>take</u>, and <u>ask</u> is the opposite of _____.

    (A) get   (B) answer   (C) teacher

3. <u>Help</u> is the opposite of <u>harm</u>, and <u>work</u> is the opposite of _____.

    (A) hurt   (B) try   (C) play

4. <u>Good</u> is the opposite of <u>bad</u>, and <u>rough</u> is the opposite of _____.

    (A) smooth   (B) bumpy   (C) mean

5. <u>Over</u> is the opposite of <u>under</u>, and <u>near</u> is the opposite of _____.

    (A) middle   (B) far   (C) here

6. <u>Warm</u> is the opposite of <u>cool</u>, and <u>safe</u> is the opposite of _____.

    (A) afraid   (B) cold   (C) unsafe

7. <u>Cloudy</u> is the opposite of <u>sunny</u>, and <u>early</u> is the opposite of _____.

    (A) late   (B) day   (C) timely

8. <u>Top</u> is the opposite of <u>bottom</u>, and <u>front</u> is the opposite of _____.

    (A) whole   (B) back   (C) side

Scholastic

nothing	everything
begin	start
fearful	afraid
woods	forest
jam	train
yard	rest
hair	hare
here	weight

wait	sunflower
bathtub	toothpaste
library	circle
square	hexagon
sum	equal
solve	continent
island	ocean
river	regroup

Vocabulary Practice Test

Fill in the bubble next to the correct answer.

1. Chose a word that you might use to describe an apple.
   - ○ **A**   smart
   - ● **B**   juicy
   - ○ **C**   pink
   - ○ **D**   tall

2. Choose a word you might use to describe your best friend.
   - ● **F**   nice
   - ○ **G**   striped
   - ○ **H**   green
   - ○ **J**   mean

3. Choose the word that is opposite of dirty.
   - ● **A**   unclean
   - ○ **B**   untidy
   - ○ **C**   clean
   - ○ **D**   rough

Vocabulary Practice Test

Fill in the bubble next to the correct answer.

4. Choose the word that means almost the same as ripped.

○ **A** broke

● **B** torn

○ **C** fixed

○ **D** open

5. A fare is the money you pay to ride on a bus. Which word that sounds like fare means to play according to the rules?

○ **F** feat

○ **G** fear

○ **H** fair

○ **J** fore

6. Which word is a compound word?

○ **A** printing

○ **B** sunflower

○ **C** libraries

○ **D** uncovered

Scholastic

Reading Skills &
Reading Comprehension

"Reading is fun!"—especially when your child understands how to use key reading skills to make meaning out of the words he or she reads. Good readers set a purpose when reading: to find the main idea, to discover important details, to find the sequence of the story, to compare and contrast story events or characters, to make inferences, predictions, or to draw conclusions. The activities in this section will familiarize your child with these key reading skills so that he or she is equipped to make meaning out of the stories and informational selections they read.

What to Do

Read the directions on each activity page with your child. Then have your child complete the activity. Then together check the work. Answers, when needed, are provided at the back of the workbook.

When your child reads the nonfiction selections, have him or her answer the questions to test his or her comprehension.

Keep On Going!

Read a book or watch a TV show with your child. At good stopping points ask questions like: What do you think will happen next? How is that character like or different from other characters in the story? Where does the story take place? Is there a problem? What is it? How is it solved? What have you learned?

When you are reading, do you get stuck on words that you don't know? Does not knowing a word make it hard to understand what you are reading? **Context clues** *can help you. Use context clues to figure out what the word is. That means think about the other words in the sentence. What clues do they give? Then ask yourself what other word would make sense there.*

What do you think the underlined word means in each sentence below? Circle the meaning that makes sense. Then rewrite each sentence using the meaning instead of the underlined word.

1. My domino has two white <u>pips</u>, and yours has five.

baby dogs   spots   long metal tubes

_____

2. A gray <u>fulmar</u> flew by the cruise ship.

lizard   swordfish   seabird

_____

3. The queen had a beautiful necklace made of <u>jasper</u>.

a green stone   yellow pudding   wet snow

_____

4. My sister is the best <u>flutist</u> in the high school band.

waitress   runner   flute player

_____

Scholastic

*The **main idea** of a story tells what the whole story is about.*

When you were in kindergarten, or maybe before that, you learned your ABCs. Letters are the building blocks of words. Words are the building blocks of sentences. We use sentences to communicate our thoughts and feelings. Each letter of the alphabet has at least one sound. Some letters have more than one sound. There are 26 letters in our alphabet. Many of our letters come from alphabets made long ago in far away places. In fact, the word **alphabet** comes from two words, **alpha** and **beta**, which are the first two letters in the Greek alphabet!

Underline the title that describes the main idea of the story above.

Playing With Blocks   All About Our Alphabet   The Greek Language

Now let's play a game using the alphabet. Read each clue below. Draw a line to the letters that sound like the correct answer.

1. **I borrowed some money from your piggy bank. _____ fifty cents.**

2. **This math is not hard. It's _____.**

3. **What did the blind man say to the doctor who made him see again? _____**

4. **What insect makes honey? _____**

5. **What does a Native American sleep in? _____**

6. **I drank all my milk. Now my glass is _____.**

7. **What kind of plant is that? _____**

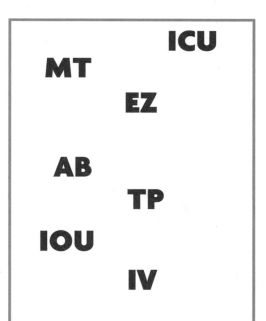

ICU

MT

EZ

AB

TP

IOU

IV

Scholastic

It is good to know that you can call a police officer when you need help. You should not be afraid of the police. Their job is to help people. Police officers help find lost children. They direct traffic when there is a problem on the roads. They arrest criminals so that our towns are safe. When people have been in car accidents, police officers come quickly to help them. During floods, fires, and tornadoes, they take people to safe places. Sometimes they rescue people who are in danger. Police officers have saved many lives. Think of a police officer as your best friend!

What do you think the main idea of this story is? To find out, read the letters that are connected in the puzzle. Write the letters in order beside the matching shapes.

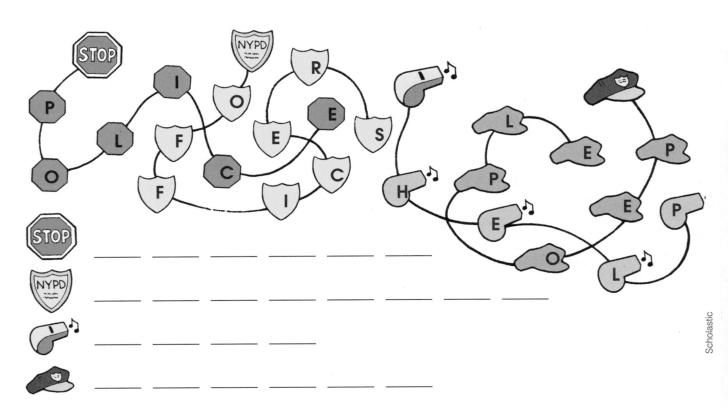

Details *are parts of a story. Details help you understand what the story is about.*

On Saturday, Rachel got up early. Her mom was still asleep, so Rachel made her own breakfast. She put some peanut butter in a bowl. She mixed it with a little honey. Then she stirred in some oatmeal, bran flakes, and raisins. It tasted yummy! When Mom got up, she said, "Oh! You made granola!"

Follow the directions below.

- **Circle the word that tells who the main character is.**

- **Underline the word that tells what day Rachel made breakfast.**

- **Put a box around the word that tells what dish Rachel put the peanut butter in.**

- **Put a star by each of the four words that tell what she mixed with the peanut butter.**

- **Put a dotted line under the word that describes how it tasted.**

- **Put two lines under the word that tells what Mom called the food.**

Now find each of the nine words from the activity above in the puzzle below and circle it. The words go across and down.

B	R	A	N	F	L	A	K	E	S	M	H	N	C	L
O	A	T	M	E	A	L	B	K	E	Q	O	J	W	I
W	R	A	I	S	I	N	S	G	R	A	N	O	L	A
L	G	S	A	T	U	R	D	A	Y	P	E	R	D	R
G	R	A	C	H	E	L	Y	U	M	M	Y	F	A	H

Gorillas are the largest apes. They live in the rain forests of Africa. Every morning, they wake up and eat a breakfast of leaves, fruit, and bark. During most of the day, the adult gorillas take naps. Meanwhile, young gorillas play. They wrestle and chase each other. They swing on vines. When the adults wake up, everyone eats again. When there is danger, gorillas stand up on their hind legs, scream, and beat their chests. Every night before it gets dark, the gorillas build a new nest to sleep in. They break off leafy branches to make their beds, either on the ground or in the trees. Baby gorillas snuggle up to their mothers to sleep.

Find the answers to the puzzle in the story. Write the answers in the squares with the matching numbers.

Across
1. During the day, adult gorillas _____.
3. Gorillas eat leaves, bark, and _____.
5. The largest apes are _____.
7. In danger, gorillas beat their _____.
8. Young gorillas swing on _____.

Down
2. The continent where gorillas live is _____.
4. When young gorillas play, they _____ and chase each other.
6. Baby gorillas snuggle up to their mothers to _____.

Scholastic

Have you ever been to a rodeo or seen one on TV? If so, you probably saw some rodeo clowns. Like clowns at a circus, they entertain the audience by doing funny tricks to make people laugh. But the main job of rodeo clowns is to protect the cowboys from the bulls. They try to catch the bull's attention long enough to allow the cowboy to escape from the arena without getting hurt. Bulls are quite fast, and they make sudden moves, so it is hard to get away from them. Angry bulls use their horns as weapons. Rodeo clowns sometimes jump in a barrel while the bull pushes it around. Other times they wave their arms or yell to keep the bull away from the cowboy. They make it look like a funny game, but it is really a very dangerous job.

Circle the letter under true or false to show your answer.

True	False		
B	Z	**1.**	Rodeo clowns do funny tricks.
R	U	**2.**	Rodeo clowns work at the circus.
L	M	**3.**	Rodeo clowns help protect the cowboys.
A	L	**4.**	Rodeo clowns distract the goats while the cowboy gets away.
R	X	**5.**	Rodeo clowns are brave.
I	V	**6.**	Bulls can make sudden moves.
F	D	**7.**	Bulls use their tails as weapons.
P	E	**8.**	Sometimes rodeo clowns jump in a cardboard box while the bull pushes it around.
R	W	**9.**	Sometimes rodeo clowns yell and wave their arms to distract the bulls.
S	C	**10.**	Rodeo clowns have a very dangerous job.

Scholastic

To find out who likes rodeo clowns, write the letters you circled in order.

____ ____ ____ ____ ____ ____ ____ ____ ____ ____

Story events that can really happen are **real**. *Story events that are make-believe are* **fantasy**.

Read each sentence below. If it could be real, circle the picture. If it is make-believe, put an *X* on the picture.

 Dairy cows give milk.

 The farmer planted pizza and hamburgers.

 The pig said, "Let's go to the dance tonight!"

 The mouse ate the dinner table.

 The hay was stacked in the barn.

 The chickens laid golden eggs.

 The green tractor ran out of gas.

 The newborn calf walked with wobbly legs.

 The goat and the sheep got married by the big tree.

 Two crickets sang "Mary Had a Little Lamb."

 Horses sat on the couch and watched TV.

 Rain made the roads muddy.

 Four little ducks swam in the pond.

 The farmer's wife baked a pumpkin pie.

Grandma Hugfuzzy lived all alone in the country. She loved to sit on the porch and watch the animals. Every day, she put food out for the rabbits and raccoons. She fed the birds with scraps of bread. She put corn out for the deer. One terrible, awful, dreadful day, Grandma Hugfuzzy's house burned down. Poor Grandma! She had nowhere to go and no one to help her. She spent the night in an old barn on a bed of hay, crying herself to sleep. During the night, the animals came to her rescue. Nine black bears chopped down some trees. A herd of deer carried the wood on their antlers. Dozens of raccoons and squirrels worked all night building a log cabin for Grandma. Birds flew above the house nailing on the roof. When morning came, Grandma Hugfuzzy was amazed to see what her animal friends had done! She threw a big party for them that lasted ten years!

Write a red *R* on things that are real. Write a purple *F* on things that are fantasy.

a woman feeding animals

deer that carry lumber

a grandmother living alone

sleeping on hay in a barn

animals building a log cabin

Home Sweet Home

WELCOME

a house burning down

bears chopping down trees

birds that can nail on a roof

crying because her house burned

a party that lasted ten years

Scholastic

Jake had a lot of homework to do. His assignment was three pages long. He added and subtracted until his hand got tired of writing.

1. What kind of homework did Jake have?

spelling   math   reading

What clues told you the answer? Underline them in the story.

After supper, Jake's dad reminded Jake to do his job. Jake went from room to room unloading baskets and cans into a large plastic bag. Then he took the bag out to the garbage can.

2. What was Jake's job?

washing dishes   making the bed   taking out the trash

What clues told you the answer? Underline them in the story.

Now Jake could have some free time. He decided to play "Star Monsters." He turned on the TV and put a cartridge in the player. He watched the monsters fighting on the TV screen while his fingers pushed buttons to make them move.

3. What was Jake doing?

playing a video game   watching the news   playing with toys

What clues told you the answer? Underline them in the story.

Jake was tired. He put on his pajamas, brushed his teeth, and crawled under the covers.

4. What was Jake doing?

waking up   getting ready for school   going to bed

What clues told you the answer? Underline them in the story.

Scholastic

Sequencing *means putting the events in a story in the order that they happened.*

Mia's black cat climbed to the top of a telephone pole and couldn't get down. "Come down, Spooky!" cried Mia. Mia thought hard. What could she do? She went across the street to ask Mr. Carson for help. He was a firefighter before he retired. "What's the matter, Mia?" asked Mr. Carson when he saw Mia's tears. "My cat is up on that pole, and I can't get her down!" Mr. Carson hugged Mia and said, "I'll call my buddies at the fire station. They will come and help." A few minutes later, Mia saw the fire truck coming. The firefighters parked near the pole and raised a long ladder to the top. A firefighter climbed the ladder and reached out for Spooky. Just then, Spooky jumped to a nearby tree limb, climbed down the tree, and ran into the backyard.
Mia said, "Spooky! You naughty cat!"
Mr. Carson and the firefighters laughed and laughed.

Read the sentences on the ladder. Number them in the order that they happen in the story.

Mia asked Mr. Carson for help.

Mr. Carson called his firefighter friends.

The firefighters laughed.

A firefighter climbed the ladder.

Mia begged Spooky to come down.

Spooky jumped to a tree and climbed down.

The fire truck came.

Mia scolded Spooky.

Scholastic

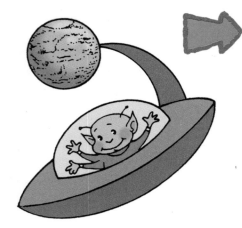

You **make inferences** *when you use story details to help you make decisions about what has happened in the story.*

Zolak boarded his spaceship and blasted off from the planet Vartog. He was on a special mission to learn about earthlings. His spaceship landed gently in a desert. Zolak walked around looking for earthlings, but all he could see were rocks and sand. Then he looked down and saw a dark creature lying down right next to him. In fact, the creature's feet were touching Zolak's feet. Zolak was scared and tried to run away, but everywhere he went, the creature followed him. At noon, Zolak realized that the creature had shrunk to a very small size but was still right next to his feet. However, during the afternoon, the dark creature grew longer and longer! Then the strangest thing happened. Night came and the dark creature completely disappeared!

1. Who do you think the dark creature was?

_____

2. Was the dark creature an earthling?   yes   no

3. Do you think Zolak will give a true report about the earthlings when he returns to Vartog?   yes   no

Why or why not?

_____

4. Draw a line to match the object to its correct shadow.

Scholastic

Read each sentence. Then color the numbered space in the picture that matches the number of the correct answer.

He rode his bike?
Who rode it?
  1. a boy
  2. a girl

Please bait my hook.
What am I doing?
  7. fishing
  8. playing baseball

Sorry! I broke it.
What could it be?
  13. a stuffed animal
  14. a crystal vase

Look at the dark cloud.
Where should you look?
  19. down
  20. up

The lamb lost its mother.
Who is its mother?
  21. a sheep
  22. a horse

She wore a red hat.
Who wore it?
  23. a man
  24. a woman

I see a thousand stars.
What time is it?
  25. noon
  26. night

Let's throw snowballs!
What time of year is it?
  3. summer
  4. winter

Breakfast is ready!
What time is it?
  9. night
  10. morning

He's a professor.
What is he?
  15. an adult
  16. a baby

Run, John, run!
What sport is John in?
  5. swimming
  6. track

I'm so thirsty.
What will I do?
  11. drink something
  12. eat something

It won't fit in the car.
What is it?
  17. a football
  18. a swing set

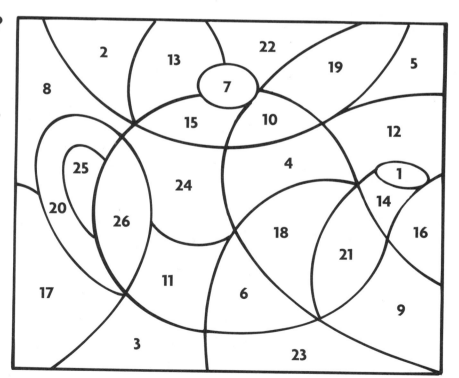

Scholastic

Classifying *means to group together things that are alike. Grouping like things together helps you see how parts of a story are connected and makes the story easier to understand.*

Last summer, Dad, Mom, Tim, and Tara went to the beach in Florida. They swam, fished, built sandcastles, and went sailing. Mom brought a picnic lunch. She spread a blanket on the sand and set out ham sandwiches, potato chips, apples, and cookies. She brought lemonade in the cooler. Later, Tim and Tara walked along the beach and saw a crab walking sideways. A stray dog was barking at it. A starfish had washed up on the beach, too. Tim threw bread crumbs up in the air to feed a flock of seagulls. Then the family went back to the hotel, and Tim and Tara played video games until bedtime.

Use the story to find the answers.
Fill in the blanks.

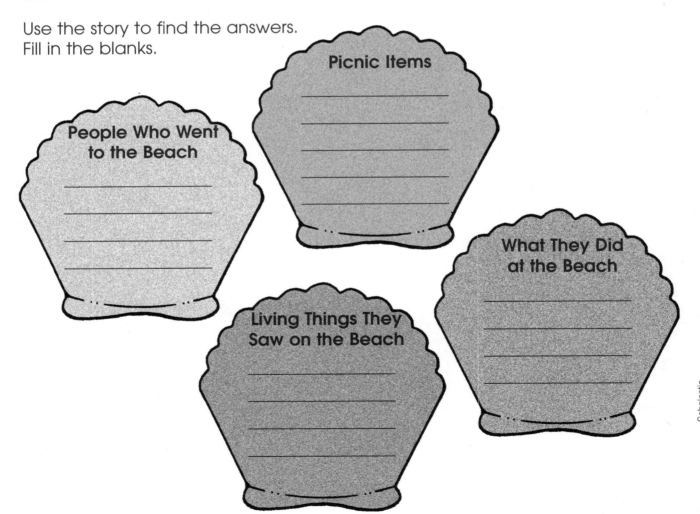

Picnic Items
_____
_____
_____
_____

People Who Went
to the Beach
_____
_____
_____
_____

What They Did
at the Beach
_____
_____
_____
_____

Living Things They
Saw on the Beach
_____
_____
_____
_____

Scholastic

Look for similarities when grouping items.

Read each list. Cross out the word that doesn't belong. Then choose a word from the kite that belongs with each list and write it in the blank.

1. grouchy   mad   cheerful   fussy   _____

2. north   away   east   south   _____

3. goat   blue jay   robin   eagle   _____

4. juice   milk   tea   mud   _____

5. hand   toy   foot   head   _____

6. David   Bob   Ronald   Sarah   _____

7. spinach   cake   cookies   pie   _____

8. glue   bicycle   pencils   scissors   _____

9. penny   nickel   quarter   marble   _____

arm
dime
George
pudding
lemonade
parakeet
crayons
angry
west

Now read these categories. In each box, write the number from the above list that matches the category.

Birds	Desserts	Bad Feelings
Boys' Names	Money	School Supplies
Directions	Body Parts	Drinks

*When you make a **prediction**, you guess what will happen next.*

Read each story. Write what you think will happen next on the lines.

1. The baseball game was tied 6–6 at the bottom of the ninth inning with bases loaded. The home team batter hit a high fly ball deep into right field. The outfielder caught the ball but then dropped it. What will happen next?

_____

_____

_____

2. Latoya decided to bake some brownies. She put them in the oven and went outside and jumped in the pool. She swam for a long time. She forgot all about the brownies. What will happen next?

_____

_____

_____

3. Mrs. Lopez ran over a big nail. It stuck in the tire. Air began to seep out. What will happen next?

_____

_____

_____

4. The wind began to blow. Dark clouds drifted in. Lightning cracked, and thunder roared. What will happen next?

_____

_____

_____

5. One day Greg left his toy truck on the stairs. Mom came down the stairs carrying a laundry basket piled high with dirty towels. She stepped on Greg's truck. What will happen next?

_____

_____

_____

6. Dad and Sam went fishing. They rowed the boat to the middle of the lake. Then they hit a rock that made a hole in the boat. Water started rushing in it. What will happen next?

_____

_____

_____

Scholastic

Once upon a time Rita Rabbit was complaining to Diana Duck. "You always have fun, swimming around in the lake. I wish I was a duck. You're lucky." Diana Duck said, "Oh, really? Well, I wish I was a rabbit! You can hop so fast and go so far. I think you're lucky!" Just then the Good Fairy appeared and said, "You are both lucky! I will grant you each your wish." All of a sudden Rita Rabbit became a duck! She waddled to the lake and went for a swim. Diana Duck became a rabbit and hopped down the road as fast as she could go. At the end of the day, Rita was wet and cold. She missed her family. She missed her home in the hole at the bottom of the hollow tree. She wanted to hop over there, but it was too far, and all she could do was waddle. Diana was having trouble, too. She had hopped so far away that she got lost. She began to cry. She wanted to go home to the lake. Just then . . . POOF! The Good Fairy appeared again. She granted Rita and Diana one more wish.

Draw what you think happened when Rita got her second wish.

Draw what you think happened when Diana got her second wish.

Scholastic

Compare *means to look for things that are the same.*
Contrast *means to look for things that are different.*

The second-grade class went to the zoo for a field trip. The next day, the teacher asked the children to write a report about what they learned. Read the two reports below.

Ryan

What I Learned at the Zoo

I learned about the giant tortoise. It was so big that the guide let us sit on its back. Some tortoises live to be over 100 years old! That's older than my grandpa!

The slowest-moving mammal is the three-toed sloth. It hangs from trees and eats fruit. Some sloths sleep more than 20 hours a day. What a lazy animal!

I thought the albino alligator was really cool. It wasn't green. It was completely white all over. It was born that way.

Jessica

What I Learned at the Zoo

The tallest animal on earth is the giraffe. It eats leaves from the tops of the trees. Giraffes come from Africa.

I learned about an albino alligator. It was white instead of green. The guide told us that it was born without the coloring of other alligators.

I saw an owl sleeping in a tree. Owls sleep in the daytime and hunt at night. When they sleep, they don't fall out of the tree because they have sharp claws that lock onto the branch.

Ryan and Jessica each wrote about three animals. Write the names of the animals they wrote about in the correct circles. In the center where both circles overlap, write the name of the animal that they both wrote about.

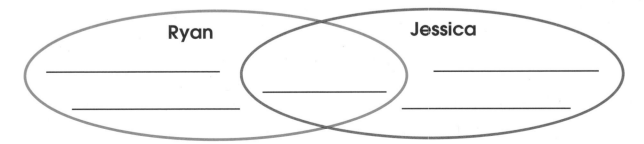

Scholastic

Kendra and her mom left their house on Oak Street to go to school. Kendra put on her safety belt. About that same time, Lacey and her mom left their house on Maple Street. On the way to school, Lacey bounced up and down on the seat watching her pigtails fly up and down in the mirror. She had forgotten to wear her safety belt.

Both moms turned into the school parking lot at the same time, and they crashed into each other! Kendra was not hurt. Her safety belt kept her in her seat. But, Lacey fell forward and bumped her head HARD! She cried and cried. She had to go to the hospital and get an X ray. Lacey got well in a day or two, but she learned an important lesson!

Draw a 😊 in the correct column.

		Kendra	Lacey	both
1.	driven to school by Mom			
2.	wore a safety belt			
3.	didn't wear a safety belt			
4.	lives on Maple Street			
5.	was in a wreck			
6.	bumped her head			
7.	got an X ray			
8.	lives on Oak Street			
9.	bounced up and down in the car			
10.	didn't get hurt			
11.	learned a lesson			

Scholastic

In a story, there is usually a reason something happens. This is the **cause**. What happened as a result is the **effect**.

It was a long way to Aunt Ruth's house. Terry and Mary Beth started getting a little bit too loud in the back seat, so Dad said, "Girls, settle down. Be quiet and read your books." They knew Dad meant business. Just then, Mary Beth saw a bee flying around in the car. Her eyes got big, and she ducked her head, swatting the bee away. Terry looked at her, and Mary Beth loudly whispered, "BEEEE!" Terry wanted to scream, but she knew Dad would get mad. "What are you two doing back there?" Dad asked. Just then, the bee landed on Dad's bald head. Mary Beth knew she had to save him from getting stung, so she whopped Dad on the head with her book. Dad jerked the steering wheel, and the car ran off the road and through a fence. The cows that were in the field ran away. Later, a police officer gave Dad a ticket for reckless driving.

Draw a line to match the cause to the effect.

The girls got too loud, so

The girls saw a bee land on Dad's bald head, so

The car ran off the road and through a fence,

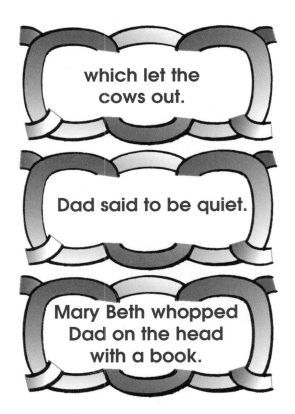

which let the cows out.

Dad said to be quiet.

Mary Beth whopped Dad on the head with a book.

Scholastic

Mount Saint Helens is an active volcano in the state of Washington. In 1980, this volcano erupted, spewing hot lava into the air. Explosions caused a huge cloud of dust. This gray dust filled the air and settled on houses and cars many miles away. The thick dust made it hard for people and animals to breathe. The explosions flattened trees on the side of the mountain. The hot rocks caused forest fires. The snow that was on the mountain melted quickly, causing floods and mud slides. Mount Saint Helens still erupts from time to time but not as powerfully as it did in 1980.

Read each phrase below. Write the number of each phrase in the top of the volcano to correctly complete the sentence.

1. **Mount Saint Helens erupted,**

2. **The thick ash made it hard**

3. **The explosions**

4. **The hot rocks caused**

5. **Melting snow caused**

6. **Because Mount Saint Helens is an active volcano,**

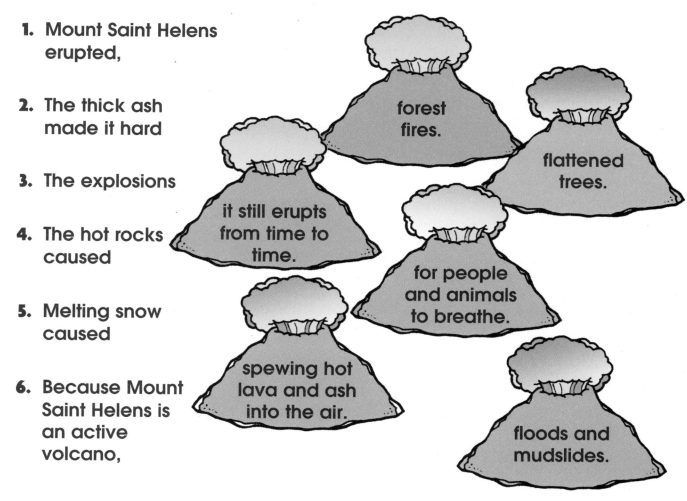

forest fires.

flattened trees.

it still erupts from time to time.

for people and animals to breathe.

spewing hot lava and ash into the air.

floods and mudslides.

*A **character** is a person or animal in a story. To understand a character better, you should pay attention to the details in the story about the character.*

Tad is a very special boy. He is confined to a wheelchair. He was born with a disease that made him unable to walk. Some boys would be sad or angry about that, but not Tad. Instead, he looks for ways to make people happy. He called the Green Oaks School for the Blind and asked if he could volunteer. They said, "Sure!" Tad went to the school and quickly made friends. Every day, he reads books to the children. He plays games with them. Sometimes he helps them do their schoolwork. The children at the school nicknamed him Lucky because they feel so lucky to have him as a friend. That makes Tad very happy!

- If Tad is confined to a wheelchair, write an H in Box 1 and Box 9. If not, write a J in both boxes.

- If Tad feels sorry for himself, write a U in Box 2 and Box 10. If he doesn't, write a E in both boxes.

- If Tad looks for ways to make people happy, write an L in Box 3. If he doesn't, write a B.

- If Tad volunteers at the River Oak School for the Blind, write a Z in Box 4. If that is not correct, write a P.

- If Tad reads to the blind children, write an N in Box 5. If not, write a V.

- If Tad plays games with the blind children, write a G in Box 6. If not, write a D.

- If Tad helps them with their homework, write an O in Box 7. If not, write an R.

- If the children nicknamed Tad "Grumpy," write a K in Box 8. If not, write a T.

- If Tad is a happy person, write an R in Box 11. If not, write a C.

This is the story of Helen Keller.

Scholastic

Tad's secret of happiness is

				I			7	8	9	10	11 S
1	2	3	4		5	6					

The writing assignment in Ms. Daniels' class was to write about someone you admire. Read what one student wrote.

Lunch Lady

by Karen Jackson

I don't know her name. She is one of the workers in our school cafeteria. I just call her Lunch Lady. She's my friend. There are several nice ladies in the cafeteria, but the Lunch Lady is the nicest of all. Every day she smiles at me when I go through the line. She says things like, "Hi Karen! Are you having a good day?" Lunch Lady always remembers that I like chicken nuggets the best. Whenever those are being served, she hands me the chicken nuggets and says, "Look, your favorite!" One day, I tripped and dropped my tray. Food went all over the floor. I was so embarrassed, but Lunch Lady came to my rescue. She helped me pick up the mess, and she told me, "Don't worry about it. It's okay." That made me feel better. Another time, I was at the shoe store with my mom, and I saw Lunch Lady. She gave me a big hug. The reason I admire Lunch Lady is because she is friendly and kind.

Read each sentence. Find the words that are wrong and cross them out. Then above them write the correct word or words that make the sentence true.

1. Karen wrote about Lunch Man.

2. Karen's favorite food is hot dogs.

3. Lunch Lady frowns when Karen comes through the line.

4. When Karen dropped her tray, Miss Daniels helped her.

5. One time, Karen saw the Lunch Lady at the hardware store.

6. Karen admires Lunch Lady because she is friendly and mean.

Scholastic

Panda Pair

In 1972, Americans fell in love with two giant pandas named Hsing-Hsing and Ling-Ling. The pandas came to the United States from China. The National Zoo in Washington, D.C., became the pandas' new home. On their first day there, 20,000 people visited the two pandas. The crowds kept coming year after year.

Hsing-Hsing and Ling-Ling were just cubs when they got to the United States. As the years passed, many hoped the pair would have cubs of their own. Ling-Ling gave birth several times. But none of the babies lived more than a few days.

Each time a cub died, people around the world felt sad.

Both pandas lived to an old age. Ling-Ling was 23 when she died in 1992. Hsing-Hsing died in 1999 at the age of 28. But the pandas were not forgotten. At the National Zoo, the glass walls of their home were covered with letters from children. The letters expressed the children's love for the pandas and told how much they were missed.

Fill in the bubble next to the correct answer.

1. The author wrote this passage mostly to

    ○ **A**   tell about Hsing-Hsing and Ling-Ling.

    ○ **B**   explain where giant pandas come from.

    ○ **C**   describe a giant panda's cubs.

    ○ **D**   convince people to visit the National Zoo.

2. According to the author, how did people feel about the pandas?

_____

3. If you visited the National Zoo in 2000, what would you have seen at the pandas' home?

_____

Scholastic

Treasure Hunt

The city of Whitingham is holding a children's treasure hunt. Children between the ages of seven and twelve may take part. The treasure hunt will take place at Benoit Park on May 31 at 1:00 P.M. Children should meet inside the park's west gate.

Treasure hunters will be given a set of ten clues that lead to the treasure. Children may hunt alone or in teams. The hidden treasure is a box filled with coupons worth $300 in all. The coupons can be used at these places:

Aggie's Ice-Cream Shop
Bike and Skate World
Feather and Fish Pet Store
Gibbons Bowling Alley
Whitingham Roller Rink
Toy City

In case of rain, the treasure hunt will take place on June 7 at 1:00 P.M.

1. Where will the treasure hunt take place?

   ○ **A** Whitingham Roller Rink   ○ **C** Gibbons Bowling Alley

   ○ **B** Toy City   ○ **D** Benoit Park

2. What is inside the hidden treasure box?

   _____

3. What will happen to the treasure hunt if it rains on May 31?

   _____

Scholastic

Bye-Bye, Fly

In a marsh somewhere in North Carolina, a hungry fly is looking for a meal. A plant called the Venus's flytrap seems like a good bet. Its leaves, which grow in pairs like a clam's shell, shine with a sweet juice. So the fly lands on a leaf. Then it takes a few steps toward the juice.

Snap! The leaves close tight around the fly. It is trapped. Now, instead of enjoying the Venus's flytrap's sweet juice, the fly will be eaten by the plant.

Of course, most plants don't eat insects. They can get all the nutrients they need from the soil. But North Carolina's marshes are missing some important nutrients. Few plants can grow there. The Venus's flytrap can, though, because it gets the nutrients it needs from the insects it eats.

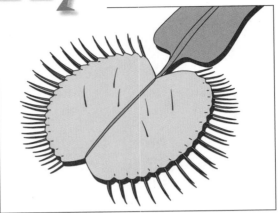

The leaves of the Venus's flytrap are covered with small hairs.

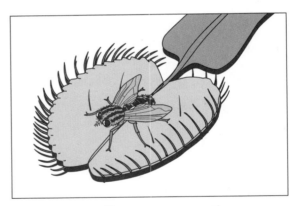

The Venus flytrap senses the insect when it touches the hairs.

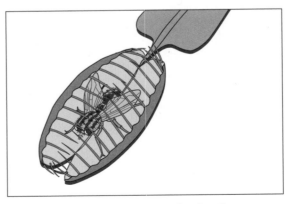

In less than a second, the leaves snap shut. The insect is trapped.

Scholastic

Fill in the bubble next to the correct answer.

1. The Venus's flytrap attracts insects because it

    ○ **A**   has leaves that grow in pairs.

    ○ **B**   smells like a clam.

    ○ **C**   has sweet juice on its leaves.

    ○ **D**   has nutrients that insects need.

2. How is the Venus's flytrap different from most plants?

    ○ **F**   It needs nutrients.

    ○ **G**   It has shiny leaves.

    ○ **H**   It grows in soil.

    ○ **J**   It eats insects.

Answer the questions on the lines.

3. Where does the Venus's flytrap grow?

_____

4. What causes the Venus's flytrap to close its leaves around an insect?

_____

5. Look at the last picture and read the sentence that goes with it. What will happen next to the insect in this picture?

_____

The Statue of Liberty

Have you ever been to New York City? There are many exciting things to see. One sight is the famous Brooklyn Bridge. It was built more than 100 years ago. Another is the Empire State Building. It is one of the tallest buildings in the world. You can take an elevator ride to the top of the building. From there, you can see for miles.

One of the best things to see in New York is the Statue of Liberty. It stands on Liberty Island in New York Harbor.

The best way to see the statue is to go to Battery Park. Stand in Battery Park looking out at the water. The Statue of Liberty is across the harbor in front of you. To the right you will see Ellis Island. Behind you is an old fort that you can explore. You can take a ferry from Battery Park to Liberty Island, if you want to see the statue up close.

The Statue of Liberty is 151 feet high. It was given to the United States by France in 1884. The statue is a woman in a long robe holding a torch, and she stands for freedom.

Since 1886, millions of people have visited the Statue of Liberty. For many people who came here by ship from other countries, the Statue of Liberty was the first thing they saw. It is an important symbol of our nation.

Fill in the bubble next to the correct answer.

1. Where is the Statue of Liberty?

○ **A**   on Ellis Island

○ **B**   in Battery Park

○ **C**   on Liberty Island

○ **D**   in Brooklyn

Answer the questions on the lines.

2. Name three famous things you can see in New York City.

_____

_____

3. Where did the Statue of Liberty come from?

_____

_____

4. Suppose you are standing in Battery Park looking out at the water. What can you see in front of you, and what is behind you?

_____

_____

_____

Reading Skills & Reading Comprehension Practice Test

Fill in the bubble next to the correct answer.

1. Which word explains the underlined word in the following sentence?
   The <u>data</u> helped to explain how the accident happened.

   A   certificate

   B   idea

   ● C   information

   D   results

2. Which sentence tells the main idea about Neil Armstrong's visit to the moon?

   F   On July 20, 1969, Neil walked on the moon.

   G   He saw rocks and moon dust.

   H   Neil Armstrong walks on the moon.

   J   Millions of people watched this amazing event.

3. Which story event is fantasy?

   A   The flower spread its beautiful petals.

   B   The horse ran free on the range.

   C   It was raining cats and dogs.

   D   Ants attacked our picnic basket.

Scholastic

Reading Skills & Reading Comprehension Practice Test

Fill in the bubble next to the correct answer.

4. Which conclusion would you draw about the following event?
Tim worked very hard. When he finished, the car sparkled in the sun.

 ○ **A** Tim made breakfast.

 ○ **B** Tim washed his car.

 ○ **C** He won the basketball game.

 ○ **D** He built a car.

5. Which event came first?

 ○ **F** Pam finished her homework.

 ○ **G** Pam went to school.

 ○ **H** She was late to school

 ○ **J** She woke up tired.

6. The temperature was falling. The leaves on the trees were turning gold and orange. What season was it?

 ○ **A** summer

 ○ **B** winter

 ○ **C** spring

 ○ **D** fall

Scholastic

Fill in the bubble next to the correct answer.

7. Which of the following words could name the group that contains the words north and east?

- ⬤ **A**   compass
- ◯ **B**   scale
- ◯ **C**   distance
- ◯ **D**   bay

8. Which of the following does NOT belong in the group?

- ◯ **F**   Lincoln
- ◯ **G**   Trump
- ◯ **H**   Washington
- ◯ **J**   Clinton

9. Which of the following does NOT belong with the others?

- ◯ **A**   tree
- ◯ **B**   leaf
- ◯ **C**   bird
- ◯ **D**   limb

Scholastic

Read the story. Then fill in the bubble next to the correct answer.

Karen has three pet fish. One fish is orange. One fish is black. One fish is red. Karen touches the water and the fish come to the top. Karen feeds her fish every day. She cleans the fishbowl each week. The water is always clean and clear. Karen's fish look very happy swimming in their bowl.

10. A good title for this story would be:

○ **A**   Karen and Her Fish

○ **B**   Karen Has A Red Fish

○ **C**   Fish Love Clean Water

○ **D**   Karen Cleans the Fish Bowl

11. Which is NOT one of the colors of Karen's fish?

○ **F**   red

○ **G**   yellow

○ **H**   black

○ **J**   orange

12. Another word for "clear" is:

○ **A**   dirty

○ **B**   old

○ **C**   clogged

○ **D**   clean

Grammar/Writing

To be successful at playing any game, you have to understand the rules of the game. The same thing is true of writing. Grammar provides the rules your child needs to become a successful writer.

The activities in this section set out the rules for writing. They start with the four types of sentences and the punctuation for each. This is the basic step to good writing. Your child will also learn the parts of speech—nouns, pronouns, adjectives, verbs—and how to use them to produce clear, interesting, and well-developed sentences.

What to Do

Each new skill starts with a definition or explanation. Have your child read the definitions or explanations on the activity page. Then have your child complete the activity. Review his or her work together. Let your child know that he or she is doing a great job!

Keep On Going!

Make learning grammar fun! Take a walk together. On your walk, play a game with your child. See who can name the greatest number of naming words they see in the neighborhood: trees, flowers, houses, Mrs. Jackson, and so on. Challenge each other to come up with the greatest number of words to describe the things you see on your walk: The tall, green, leafy oak tree is next to the small, green house on the corner of Maine and King Streets.

noun   **adjective**   **verb**

*A **telling sentence** tells something. It begins with a capital letter and ends with a period. A **question** asks something. It begins with a capital letter and ends with a question mark.*

Read each sentence. Write T on the line if the sentence is a telling sentence. Write Q on the line if it is a question.

1 I took my pet to see the vet. _T_

2 Was your pet sick? _Q_

3 What did the vet do? _Q_

4 The vet checked my pet. _T_

5 The vet said my pet had a cold. _T_

**The order of the words in a sentence can change its meaning.
Write T next to the sentence that is a telling sentence.
Write Q next to the sentence that is a question.**

6 Is your pet well now? _Q_

7 Now your pet is well. _T_

Scholastic

An **exclamation** *shows strong feelings, such as excitement, surprise, or fear. It begins with a capital letter and ends with an exclamation mark (!).*

A **command** *makes a request or tells someone to do something. It ends with a period or an exclamation mark.*

Read each exclamation. Use words from the box to tell what strong feeling it shows.

| excitement | fear | anger | surprise |

1 I lost my jacket. I'll be so cold! _____

2 Look what I have! _____

3 I didn't know you had my jacket! _____

4 Give it to me now! _____

Look at the picture.

5 Circle the command that goes with the picture.

Please don't be upset!   Wear your new hat.

6 Write another command for the picture.

_____

7 Write an exclamation for the picture.

_____

Scholastic

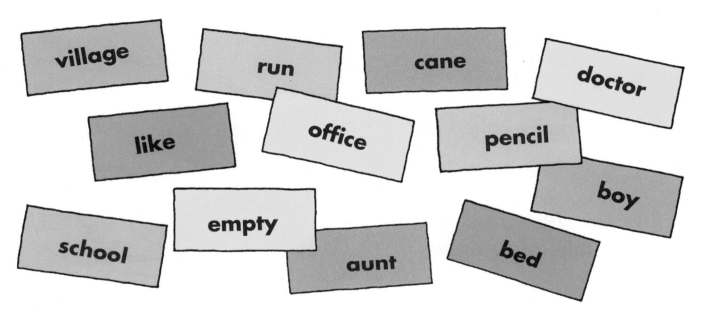

Common nouns *name people, places, or things.*

Help sort the cards. Some of the words are nouns. Some are not. Circle the nouns.

village

run

cane

doctor

like

office

pencil

boy

school

empty

aunt

bed

Write each noun you circled under the correct heading.

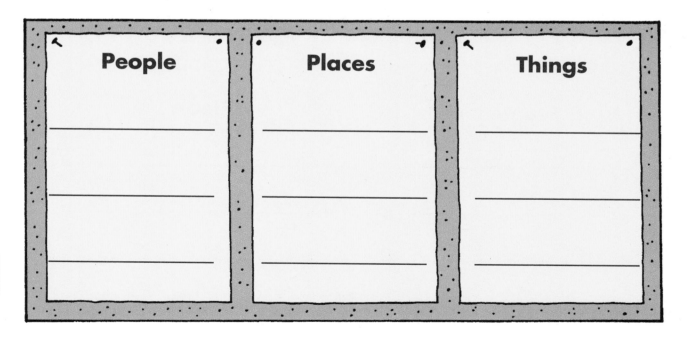

People	Places	Things

Proper nouns *are special names of people and places. They are always capitalized.*

Read each sentence. Circle the proper noun.

1 George Ancona is a photographer.

2 He was born in Mexico.

3 His family called him Jorgito.

4 They lived in Coney Island.

5 Now he travels to Honduras to take pictures.

6 Tio Mario worked in a sign shop.

Write the proper nouns you circled under the correct heading below.

People   **Places**

_____   _____

_____   _____

_____   _____

*Most nouns add **-s** to mean more than one. Nouns that end in **s**, **x**, **ch**, or **sh** add **-es** to mean more than one.*

Read each sentence. Add *-s* or *-es* to the noun at the end of the sentence to make it plural. Write it in the sentence.

1 **Dad made five cheese** _____. (sandwich)

2 **He packed five** _____ **for the children.** (lunch)

3 **Lisa put fruit in all the** _____. (lunchbox)

4 **She packed some paper** _____, **too.** (dish)

Write the plural for each noun on the line.

5 **one box**

two _____

6 **one dress**

two _____

7 **one coat**

two _____

8 **one bench**

two _____

Scholastic

A **pronoun** *takes the place of the name of a person, place, or thing.*

Read the story. Use the pronouns in the box to complete each sentence. The first one has been done for you.

| they   he   she   it |

Glenda was walking in the woods. At last ___she___

came to a house. _____ was empty. She opened the
                        1

door and saw three chairs by the fireplace. _____
                                                2

were all different sizes. She sat down on the smallest one.

_____ was the perfect size for her. Soon _____
    3   4

fell asleep. When she woke up, three pigs were

standing over her. The father pig spoke. _____
                                              5

asked Glenda if she would stay for dinner. "I would love

to!" said Glenda.

Scholastic

A **verb** *is an action word. It tells what someone or something is doing.*

Read each sentence. Write the action verb on the line.

1. Ronald runs to the field. _____

2. Michael wears a batting helmet. _____

3. He smacks the ball hard. _____

4. Ronald holds the wrong end of the bat. _____

5. He misses the ball. _____

6. Ronald waits in left field. _____

7. He writes *G* for great. _____

8. Ronald's father helps him. _____

Write a sentence about the picture.
Use an action verb and circle it.

_____

_____

*Some verbs add **-ed** to tell about actions that happened in the past.*

Read the first sentence in each pair. Change the underlined verb to tell about the past.

1 Today my dogs <u>push</u> open the back door.

Yesterday my dogs _____ open the back door.

2 Today they <u>splash</u> in the rain puddles.

Last night they _____ in the rain puddles.

3 Now they <u>roll</u> in the mud.

Last week they _____ in the mud.

4 Today I <u>follow</u> my dogs' footprints.

Last Sunday I _____ my dogs' footprints.

5 Now I <u>wash</u> my dogs from head to toe.

Earlier I _____ my dogs from head to toe.

Write a sentence using one of the verbs you wrote.

_____

_____

_____

Scholastic

Am, **is**, **are**, **was**, *and* **were** *are forms of the verb* **to be**. *These verbs show being instead of action.*

Read each sentence. Underline the verb. Write *past* if the sentence tells about the past. Write *now* if the sentence tells about the present.

1 **The story is perfect.** _____

2 **The producers are happy.** _____

3 **The actors were funny.** _____

4 **The movie studio is interested in the story.** _____

5 **I am excited about the movie.** _____

6 **I was sad at the end.** _____

Irregular verbs change their spelling when they tell about the past. **Did** *is the past form of* **do** *and* **does**. **Went** *is the past form of* **go** *and* **goes**.

Read each sentence. Write *present* if the underlined verb tells about action now. Write *past* if it tells about action in the past.

Present	Past
go, goes	went
do, does	did

1 Grace <u>goes</u> to the playground.   _____

2 Some other children <u>go</u>, too.   _____

3 Grace <u>does</u> a scene from a story.   _____

4 The children <u>do</u> the scene with her.   _____

5 Grace <u>went</u> into battle as Joan of Arc.   _____

6 She <u>did</u> the part of Anansi the
Spider, too.   _____

7 In another part, Grace <u>went</u> inside
a wooden horse.   _____

8 She <u>did</u> many other parts.   _____

Scholastic

*The verb **have** is irregular. Use **have** or **has** to tell about the present. Use **had** to tell about the past.*

Choose the correct word from the chart to complete each sentence.

In the Present	In the Past
have, has	had

1 Now, Joe _____ new running shoes.

2 I _____ new shoes now, too.

3 Last week we _____ old shoes.

4 I _____ a green shirt on now.

5 Joe _____ a blue shirt on now.

6 Yesterday we both _____ red shirts on.

7 Last year we _____ to walk to the park.

8 Now, I _____ skates.

9 Now, Joe _____ a bike.

Scholastic

An **adjective** describes a person, place, or thing. Color, size, and number words are adjectives.

Read each sentence. Underline the nouns. Write the adjective that tells about each noun.

1 The brown donkey carried the heavy pack.

_____ _____

2 The striped cat chased two birds.

_____ _____

3 The little rooster crowed six times.

_____ _____

Write the adjectives from the sentences above.

4 Write the adjectives that tell what kind.

_____

5 Write the adjectives that tell how many.

_____

Scholastic

> **Quotation marks** *show the exact words someone says. They go before the speaker's first word. They also go after the speaker's last word and the end punctuation mark.*

Read each sentence. Underline the exact words the speaker says. Put the words in quotation marks. The first one has been done for you.

1 Max said, "Let's go on a picnic."

2 Cori replied,   That's a great idea.

3 Andy asked,   What should we bring?

4 Max said with a laugh,   We should bring food.

5 Cori added,   Yes, let's bring lots and lots of food.

6 Andy giggled and said,   You're no help at all!

Finish the sentences below by writing what Max, Cori, and Andy might say next. Use quotation marks.

7 Max said, _____.

8 Cori asked, _____.

9 Andy answered, _____.

Scholastic

A **contraction** consists of two words made into one word. An apostrophe takes the place of the missing letter or letters. In a contraction, **not** becomes **n't**.

Read each sentence. Underline the contraction. Write the two words it is made from.

1 The little old man and little old woman aren't ready. _____

2 The Gingerbread Man doesn't want to be eaten. _____

3 They can't catch him. _____

4 They couldn't run fast enough. _____

5 He didn't come back. _____

6 The Gingerbread Man isn't afraid of the fox. _____

Draw a line to match each contraction to the two words it is made from.

7 hadn't   were not

8 don't   had not

9 weren't   do not

If the naming part of a sentence names one, add -s to the action word. If the naming part names more than one, do not add -s to the action word.

Read each sentence. Write the word in parentheses ( ) that correctly completes it on the line.

1 Kim _____ a story about a monkey. (write, writes)

2 The monkey _____ his friend in the city. (meet, meets)

3 The two friends _____ on the bus. (ride, rides)

4 The monkeys _____ for toys and presents. (shop, shops)

5 The store _____ at 7 o'clock. (close, closes)

6 The monkeys _____ the time. (forget, forgets)

7 The owner _____ the door. (lock, locks)

8 The friends _____ on the window. (bang, bangs)

9 Many people _____ for help. (call, calls)

10 Finally the monkeys _____ the door open. (hear, hears)

*You can use adjectives to compare things. To compare two things, add **-er** to the adjective. To compare three or more things, add **-est**.*

Biddie Bird has a friend named Betty. Betty always wants to outdo Biddie. If Biddie has a *clean* nest, Betty has a *cleaner* nest. Biddie and Betty have another friend named Birdie. She likes to outdo both Biddie and Betty. So she has the *cleanest* nest.

Read the sentences. Then fill in the chart so the correct form of each adjective is under each bird's name.

Biddie	Betty	Birdie
clean	cleaner	cleanest
1. _____	_____	_____
2. _____	_____	_____
3. _____	_____	_____
4. _____	_____	_____
5. _____	_____	_____
6. _____	_____	_____

1. Betty's nest is <u>newer</u> than Biddie's.

2. Biddie has a <u>small</u> nest.

3. Birdie has the <u>warmest</u> nest of all.

4. Biddie's nest is <u>round</u>.

5. Birdie built the <u>neatest</u> nest.

6. Betty has a <u>softer</u> nest than Biddie.

Scholastic

Add an apostrophe (') and an **s** to a noun to show ownership. For example, **Joe** + **'s** = **Joe's** suitcase.

Joe is packing for a trip. He needs to pack everything on the list. Each object belongs to a different family member. Study the picture to learn who owns each item. Then write the item and who owns it on the lines. The first one has been done for you.

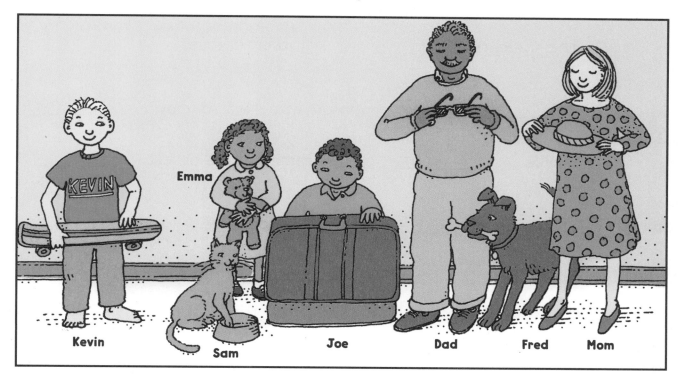

skateboard   hat   bone

bowl   sunglasses   teddy bear

1. Kevin's skateboard   4. _____

2. _____   5. _____

3. _____   6. _____

The meaning of a word often depends on how the word is used. Some words can be used as both verbs and nouns.

Add the word at the left to each sentence pair. Write *verb* or *noun* on the line next to each sentence to show how you used the word.

peel   **1.** The _____ is the cover of an orange.   _____

         2. The students _____ their oranges.   _____

ride   **3.** Jan's _____ on the camel was bumpy.   _____

         4. People _____ on camels in the desert.   _____

color   **5.** The twins _____ their pictures.   _____

         6. That _____ fades in the sun.   _____

smell   **7.** The men _____ smoke.   _____

         8. The _____ of flowers fills the air.   _____

lock   **9.** The _____ on the box is old.   _____

         10. The Turners _____ their door at night.   _____

Scholastic

The meaning of a word often depends on how the word is used. Some words can be used as both adjectives and nouns.

What is **orange**?

The fruit is a noun.
The color is an adjective.

The <u>orange</u> is on the table.
The <u>orange</u> cat hissed.

Read each sentence. Decide if the word in the box is a noun or an adjective. If the word is an adjective, color the box with the same color crayon.

1. She wore a ⬚peach⬚ dress to the party.

2. My ⬚gold⬚ ring shines.

3. I got a ⬚tan⬚ at the beach.

4. Her ⬚violet⬚ shirt matched her skirt.

5. I picked a ⬚peach⬚ from the tree.

6. ⬚Silver⬚ is a metal.

7. ⬚Violets⬚ grow in our yard.

8. The miners found ⬚gold⬚ .

9. Molly's ⬚silver⬚ pin broke.

10. A ⬚tan⬚ horse grazed in the field.

For each of these words, write two sentences. Use the word as an adjective in one sentence and a noun in the other.

square

_____

_____

cold

_____

_____

*Some sentences include a list. A **comma** (,) is used to separate each item in the list.*

Write a sentence that includes a list of the words that are given.

**coat
hat
gloves**

1. _____

_____

2. _____

_____

**spelling
reading
math**

**bread
peanut butter
jelly**

3. _____

_____

4. _____

_____

**birds
flowers
butterflies**

A sentence is more interesting when it includes a subject, an action, and a part that tells where or when.

Write three sentences and draw pictures to match.

subject	action	where or when

1. _____

subject	action	where or when

2. _____

subject	action	where or when

3. _____

*Two sentences that share the same subject can be combined to make one sentence by using the word **and**.*

Rewrite the sentences by combining their endings.

1. The party was fun.
   The party was exciting.

The party was fun and exciting

2. We blew up orange balloons.
   We blew up red balloons.

3. We ate cake.
   We ate ice cream.

4. The cake frosting was green.
   The cake frosting was yellow.

5. We made a bookmark.
   We made a clay pot.

6. We brought games.
   We brought prizes.

Scholastic

Two sentences that share the same ending can be combined to make one sentence.

Rewrite the sentences by combining their subjects.

1. **These peanuts are salty!**
These pretzels are salty!

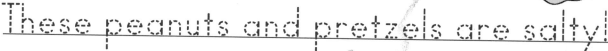
These peanuts and pretzels are salty!

2. **The first graders eat lunch at noon.**
The second graders eat lunch at noon.

_____

3. **The napkins are on the table.**
The forks are on the table.

_____

4. **Are the muffins in the oven?**
Are the cookies in the oven?

_____

5. **Michael bought lunch today.**
Stephen bought lunch today.

Mike

_____

*The **setting** of a story tells when or where it is happening.*

Imagine that you are writing a story for each picture below. How will you describe the setting? Write a sentence describing each setting.

setting	→	characters	→	problem	→	solution

It was a hot morning in the desert.

Scholastic

The people or animals in a story are called **characters**.

Some characters are likable and others are not. Write a describing sentence about each character. Be sure to give each character a name.

setting	→	characters	→	problem	→	solution

_____

_____

_____

_____

_____

_____

_____

_____

_____

Scholastic

 To make a story exciting, one of the characters often runs into a **problem**.

Think about each character in the sentences below. What could happen that would make a problem for that character? Write the next sentence creating a problem.

setting $\longrightarrow$ characters $\longrightarrow$ problem $\longrightarrow$ solution

1. Beauty Butterfly was enjoying the warm spring day.

_____

2. Jesse was supposed to wear shoes outside.

_____

3. Gabby could not wait to bite into her apple.

_____

4. Ben smacked the baseball into the air.

_____

5. Barney Bass had never seen such a big worm!

_____

Scholastic

*At the end of a story, the problem is usually solved. This is called the **solution**.*

Read the beginning and middle parts of the stories below. Write an ending solution for each.

| setting | → | characters | → | problem | → | solution |

David and his dog, Spot, were best friends. They went everywhere together. At bedtime, David whistled for Spot to jump in his bed. One winter night, David whistled and whistled, but Spot did not come.

_____

_____

Josh loved second grade, but he did not like recess. Josh's class was always the last one out to the playground. Every day, Josh ran to get a swing, but they were always taken.

_____

_____

Scholastic

Grammar/Writing Practice Test

Fill in the bubble next to the correct answer.

1. Which type of sentence is the following?
   Give me that apple.
   - ○ A   telling
   - ○ B   question
   - ○ C   exclamation
   - ○ D   command

2. Which type of sentence is the following?
   I would like to have another piece of cake.
   - ○ F   telling
   - ○ G   question
   - ○ H   exclamation
   - ○ J   command

3. Which type of sentence is the following?
   Are those bananas ripe?
   - ○ A   telling
   - ○ B   question
   - ○ C   exclamation
   - ○ D   command

Grammar/Writing Practice Test

Fill in the bubble next to the correct answer.

4. Which of the following is NOT a proper noun?

○ **A**   Emilio

○ **B**   Florida

○ **C**   Disney World

○ **D**   brother

5. Which of the following is a common noun?

○ **F**   park

○ **G**   Pat

○ **H**   Dr. Smith

○ **J**   Ridgedale Avenue

6. Which pronoun would take the place of *mom*?

○ **A**   it

○ **B**   he

○ **C**   she

○ **D**   they

Grammar/Writing Practice Test

Fill in the bubble next to the correct answer.

7. Which word correctly completes the following sentence?
   Two friends _____ beautiful necklaces.
   - **A** make
   - **B** makes
   - **C** maked
   - **D** mades

8. Which word correctly completes the following sentence?
   The boy _____ the necklace with square beads.
   - **F** pick
   - **G** picks
   - **H** picking
   - **J** pickes

9. Which word in the following sentence is an adjective?
   In the morning, Jenny put on red shoes.
   - **A** put
   - **B** shoes
   - **C** red
   - **D** on

Scholastic

Grammar/Writing Practice Test

Fill in the bubble next to the correct answer.

10. Look at the underlined verb in the following sentence. Then choose the correct form of the verb to replace it.

Last Saturday, I <u>visit</u> John in the country.

○ **A**   visits

○ **B**   visited

○ **C**   will visit

○ **D**   correct as is

11. Which punctuation is missing from the following sentence?

My favorite colors are green yellow and purple.

○ **F**   question mark

○ **G**   exclamation point

○ **H**   commas

○ **J**   period

12. Which part of a story tells where the story takes place?

○ **A**   characters

○ **B**   problem

○ **C**   solution

○ **D**   setting

Scholastic

Addition

Understanding basic addition facts is an important real-life skill. When you buy things you need to add to figure out how much money you'll need to make your purchases. Or if you want to figure out the perimeter of something, you have to add the length of each side. We probably add something every day. The addition activities that follow will give your child lots of practice in this important skill.

What to Do

These activity pages provide many opportunities for your child to practice addition with and without regrouping. When you regroup, you carry over from the right-hand column to the left-hand column. For example:

$$\begin{array}{r} {}^{1}19 \\ +\ 5 \\ \hline 24 \end{array}$$

Check your child's work when he or she finishes each activity page. For your convenience, you will find the answers at the back of the workbook.

Keep On Going!

Encourage your child to become an "addition champion." Have him or her add everything in sight: number of canned vegetables on the shelf plus number of canned fruit, number of red cars on the road plus number of blue cars, and so on.

$$2 + 3 = 5$$

Add. Complete the puzzle using number words.

1. T e n

2. F o u r

3. S e v e n

6. e g h i t

7.

Across

1. 5 + 5 = 10
2. 3 + 4 = 7
3. 2 + 7 = 9
6. 6 + 2 = 8
7. _____ + 0 = 1

Down

1. 4 + _____ = 6
2. 2 + _____ = 7
3. _____ + 4 = 10
4. 4 + 5 = _____
5. 5 + _____ = 8

Finish each number sentence with a number word.

five + two = _____   three + six = _____

Add.

Add!

1. **7 + 5 =** 2. **5 + 9 =** 3. **8 + 4 =**

4. **5 + 3 =** 5. **9 + 5 =** 6. **8 + 8 =**

7. **3 + 7 =** 8. **8 + 9 =** 9. **4 + 0 =** 10. **3 + 3 =**

11. **2 + 1 =** 12. **9 + 3 =** 13. **4 + 6 =** 14. **8 + 7 =**

15. **3 + 8 =** 16. **2 + 4 =** 17. **7 + 6 =** 18. **9 + 2 =**

19. **6 + 12 =** 20. **7 + 8 =**

Add.

Add these!

1. 7
   + 5

2. 5
   + 5

3. 9
   + 9

4. 6
   + 4

5. 6
   + 7

6. 6
   + 6

7. 2
   + 8

8. 9
   + 8

9. 8
   + 7

10. 9
    + 4

11. 2
    + 9

12. 8
    + 6

13. 5
    + 9

14. 7
    + 7

15. 10
    + 8

16. 8
    + 4

17. 9
    + 7

18. 7
    + 6

19. 3
    + 6

20. 7
    + 8

Add.

Add!

1. 6
    +4

2. 7
    +3

3. 9
    +6

4. 5
    +7

5. 7
    +8

6. 7
    +7

7. 4
    +9

8. 9
    +9

9. 5
    +8

10. 8
     +8

11. 8
     +7

12. 6
     +9

13. 8
     +6

14. 9
     +5

15. 6
     +8

16. 7
     +7

17. 4
     +9

18. 5
     +8

19. 9
     +0

20. 6
     +9

Add.

Add!

1.   6
   + 7

2.   8
   + 5

3.   7
   + 7

4.   9
   + 6

5.   5
   + 5

6.   9
   + 7

7.   6
   + 4

8.   8
   + 4

9.   9
   + 9

10.   5
    + 6

11.   6
    + 3

12.   7
    + 4

13.   8
    + 6

14.   7
    + 6

15.   7
    + 5

16.   9
    + 5

17.   8
    + 7

18.   9
    + 3

19.   8
    + 2

20.   9
    + 4

In each row, give the number that comes next.

1.	2	4	6	8	10	12	14	16	
2.	1	3	1	3	1	3	1	3	
3.	1	2	3	4	5	6	7	8	
4.	1	2	2	1	2	2	1	2	
5.	0	6	5	0	6	5	0	6	
6.	2	4	6	2	4	6	2	4	
7.	100	101	102	103	104	105	106		

In each row, give the number that comes next.

1.	5	10	15	20	25	30	35	
2.	15	14	13	12	11	10	9	
3.	1	3	2	4	1	3	2	4	1	
4.	0	5	2	0	5	2	0	5	
5.	1	4	1	4	1	4	1	4	
6.	10	20	30	40	50	60	70	
7.	3	6	9	12	15	18	21	

Add. Write the sum on each bowl.

1.

2.

3.

4.

5.

6.

7.

8.

9.

Scholastic

Why doesn't Scarecrow Sam tell secrets when he is near Farmer Joe's bean patch? _____

To find out the answer, add the numbers. Circle the pumpkins that have sums of 14, and write the letters that appear inside those pumpkins in order in the boxes below.

1. 4 + 2   G
2. 7 + 7   B
3. 9 + 5   E
4. 10 + 4   A
5. 4 + 8   R
6. 6 + 8   N
7. 11 + 3   S
8. 14 + 0   T
9. 7 + 2   P
10. 13 + 1   A
11. 5 + 8   S
12. 12 + 2   L
13. 7 + 4   H
14. 5 + 9   K

1. Solve the problems.

2. Find each number pair on the graph. Make a dot for each.

3. Connect the dots in the order that you make them.

4. What picture did you make?

_____

	Across	Up
1.	20 + 7 = _____	12 + 12 = _____
2.	12 + 3 = _____	11 + 13 = _____
3.	1 + 2 = _____	10 + 14 = _____
4.	13 + 2 = _____	10 + 5 = _____
5.	13 + 14 = _____	21 + 3 = _____
6.	23 + 4 = _____	11 + 4 = _____
7.	5 + 22 = _____	2 + 4 = _____
8.	3 + 12 = _____	1 + 5 = _____
9.	3 + 0 = _____	6 + 0 = _____
10.	2 + 1 = _____	2 + 13 = _____
11.	0 + 3 = _____	2 + 22 = _____

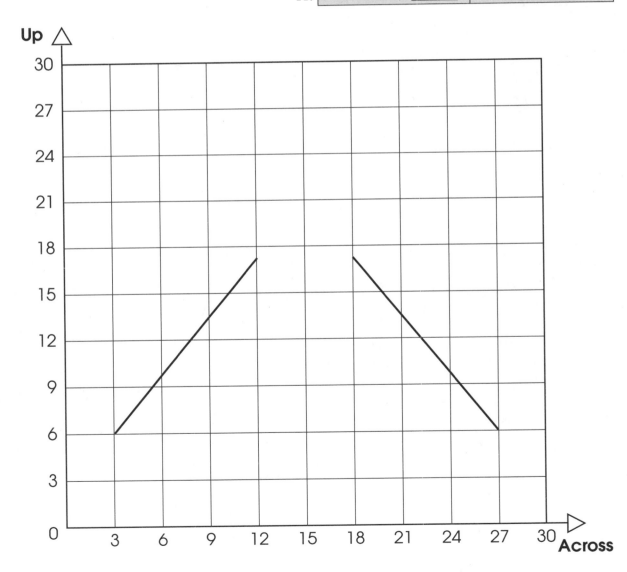

Scholastic

Add. Then use the code to write a letter in each oval to find the "good manner" words.

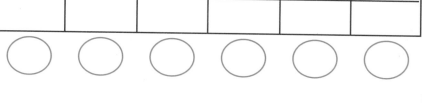

11 + 10	62 + 31	44 + 34	41 + 5	13 + 31	35 + 43

◯ ◯ ◯ ◯ ◯ ◯

40 + 10	43 + 24	42 + 4	54 + 25	41 + 42

◯ ◯ ◯ ◯ ◯

57 + 2	22 + 3	34 + 32

◯ ◯ ◯

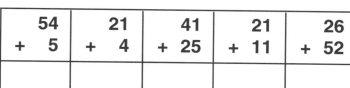

54 + 5	21 + 4	41 + 25	21 + 11	26 + 52

◯ ◯ ◯ , ◯ ◯

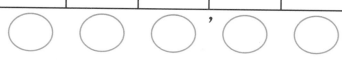

50 + 30	70 + 8	50 + 43	11 + 7	15 + 10	31 + 4	17 + 61

◯ ◯ ◯ ◯ ◯ ◯ ◯

Code

18 C	21 P	25 O	32 R	35 M	44 S	46 A	50 T
59 Y	66 U	67 H	78 E	79 N	80 W	83 K	93 L

Scholastic

Add.

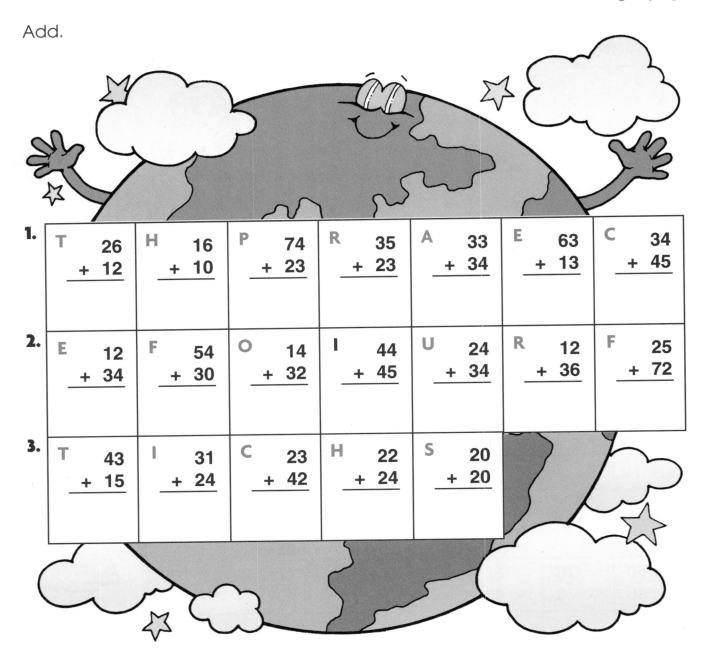

1.	T 26 + 12	H 16 + 10	P 74 + 23	R 35 + 23	A 33 + 34	E 63 + 13	C 34 + 45
2.	E 12 + 34	F 54 + 30	O 14 + 32	I 44 + 45	U 24 + 34	R 12 + 36	F 25 + 72
3.	T 43 + 15	I 31 + 24	C 23 + 42	H 22 + 24	S 20 + 20		

4. For each sum that is an even number, write its letter below in order.

How much of the earth is covered by water?

___ ___ ___ ___ — ___ ___ ___ ___ ___ ___

5. For each sum that is an odd number, write its letter below in order.

What is the biggest ocean?

___ ___ ___ ___ ___

Scholastic

Add. Connect the flowers with the same sum.

1. 43 + 26

2. 18 + 70

3. 11 + 34

4. 62 + 35

5. 13 + 12

6. 52 + 36

7. 23 + 22

8. 51 + 18

9. 14 + 11

10. 55 + 42

Add. Use the code to write words that tell about our past.

63 + 12	12 + 11	65 + 33	62 + 24	34 + 13	24 + 10	41 + 34	53 + 46

◯ ◯ ◯ ◯ ◯ ◯ ◯ ◯

40 + 46	26 + 72	23 + 10	35 + 43	21 + 43	53 + 34	22 + 10	13 + 34	64 + 14	68 + 31

◯ ◯ ◯ ◯ ◯ ◯ ◯ ◯ ◯ ◯

31 + 33	25 + 22	21 + 30	44 + 54	76 + 10	21 + 11	11 + 10

◯ ◯ ◯ ◯ ◯ ◯ ◯

40 + 11	35 + 63	44 + 20	52 + 12

◯ ◯ ◯ ◯

Code

21 Y	23 M	32 T	33 V	34 C	42 P	47 I	51 B
64 L	69 D	75 A	78 O	86 R	87 U	98 E	99 N

Scholastic

Add. Then circle each box with an odd sum to help the boy find his way to the book. Hint: Remember to look in the ones place.

1.

47 + 24	74 + 19	78 + 12	15 + 37

2.

48 + 44	31 + 59	52 + 39	29 + 57	73 + 19

3.

63 + 18	14 + 67	57 + 16	24 + 18	63 + 29

4.

57 + 28	27 + 47	76 + 16	72 + 18	76 + 18

5.

32 + 19	17 + 24	55 + 38	32 + 49	

Scholastic

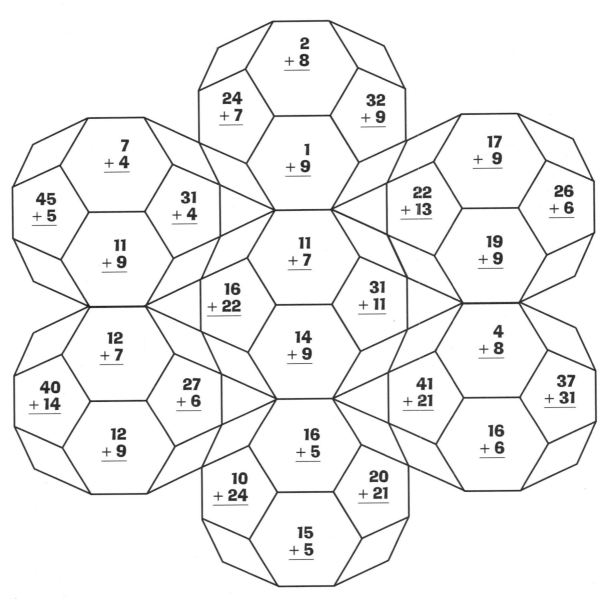

Solve the problems.

If the answer is between 1 and 30, color the shape red.

If the answer is between 31 and 99, color the shape gray.

Finish by coloring the other shapes with the colors of your choice.

Extra: Name two numbers that when added together equal 27.

_____ + _____ = _____   _____ + _____ = _____

adding multiple addends

Find the sums of the three addends in the rows across and down. The answer circles are numbered.

You can do it!

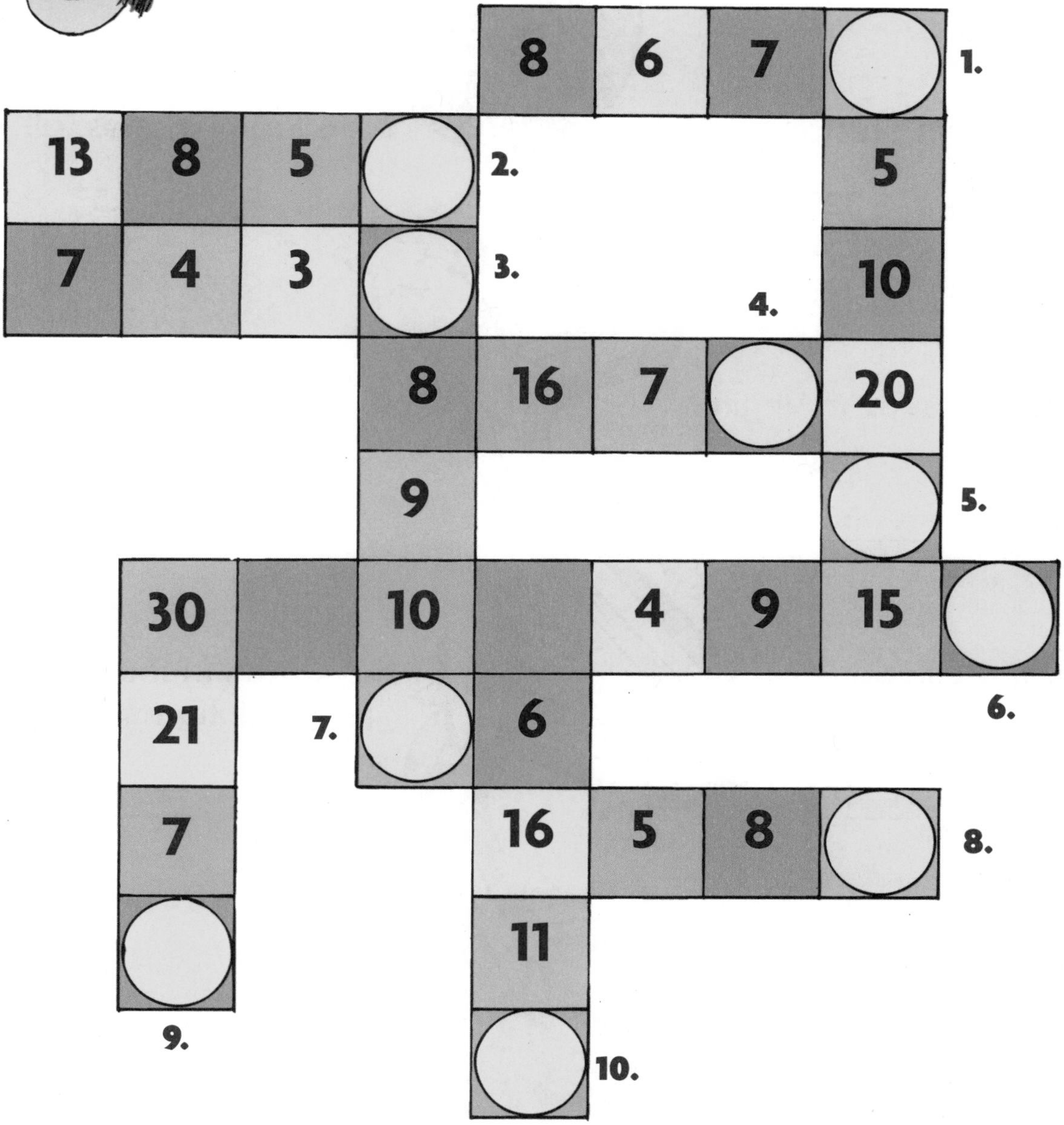

8 6 7 ◯ 1.

13 8 5 ◯ 2.   5

7 4 3 ◯ 3.   10

8 16 7 ◯ 20

9   ◯ 5.

30 10 4 9 15 ◯

21   7. ◯ 6   6.

7   16 5 8 ◯ 8.

◯   11

9.   ◯ 10.

Scholastic

Reading & Math • Grade 2 211

Add. Circle each even sum to learn about George Washington. Draw a square around each odd sum to learn about Abe Lincoln. Hint: Look in the ones place.

A. the "Father of the Country"

```
  423
+ 173
```

B. born in 1809 in Kentucky

```
  384
+ 611
```

C. sixteenth president

```
  325
+ 552
```

D. 6 feet 4 inches tall

```
  257
+ 312
```

E. born in 1732 in Virginia

```
  101
+ 561
```

F. studied geography

```
  570
+ 408
```

G. first president

```
  805
+ 163
```

H. leader in the
Revolutionary War

```
  445
+ 151
```

I. loved reading books

```
  609
+ 290
```

J. leader in the Civil War

```
  314
+ 183
```

Scholastic

Look at the number on each chick. Write the number of tens and ones on the egg. Then trade one ten for ten ones.

35

_3_ tens   _5_ ones

_2_ tens
_15_ ones

47

___ tens   ___ ones

___ tens
___ ones

82

___ tens   ___ ones

___ tens
___ ones

94

___ tens   ___ ones

___ tens
___ ones

61

___ tens   ___ ones

___ tens
___ ones

90

___ tens   ___ ones

___ tens
___ ones

Circle each group of 10. Write the number of tens and ones on the chart.
Then write the number on the baseball glove.

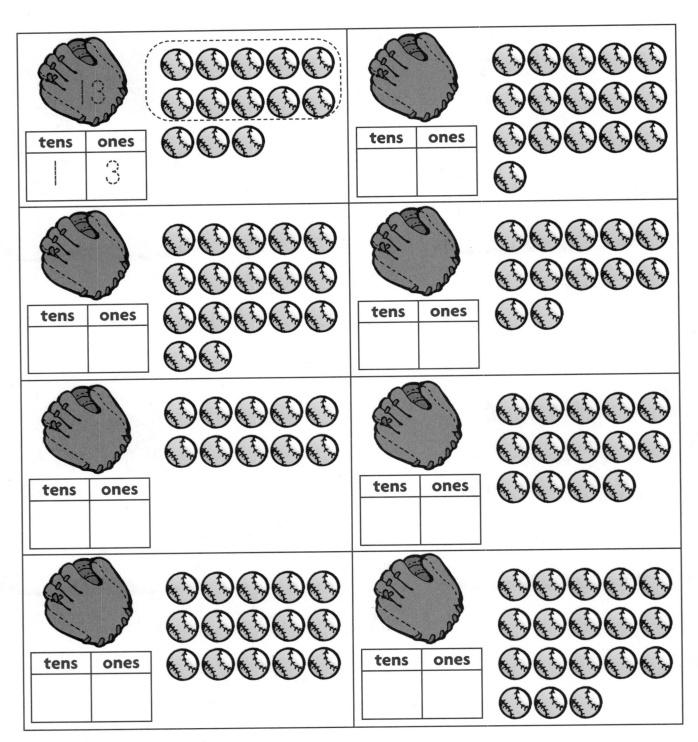

Scholastic

Regroup tens into hundreds. Remember: 10 tens = 1 hundred. Write the number of hundreds and the number of remaining tens.

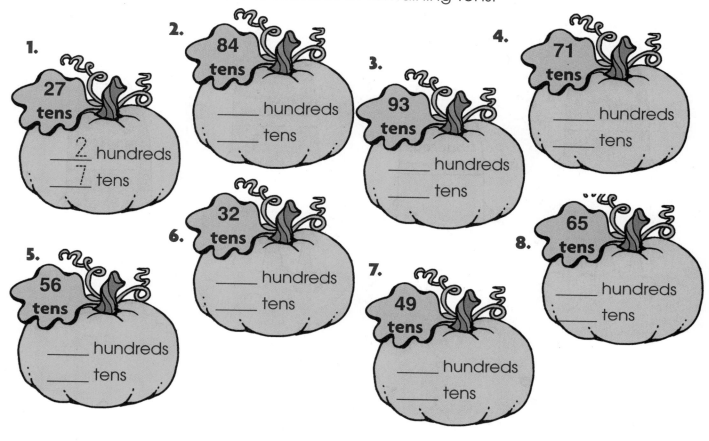

1. **27 tens**
_2_ hundreds
_7_ tens

2. **84 tens**
_____ hundreds
_____ tens

3. **93 tens**
_____ hundreds
_____ tens

4. **71 tens**
_____ hundreds
_____ tens

5. **56 tens**
_____ hundreds
_____ tens

6. **32 tens**
_____ hundreds
_____ tens

7. **49 tens**
_____ hundreds
_____ tens

8. **65 tens**
_____ hundreds
_____ tens

Write the number.

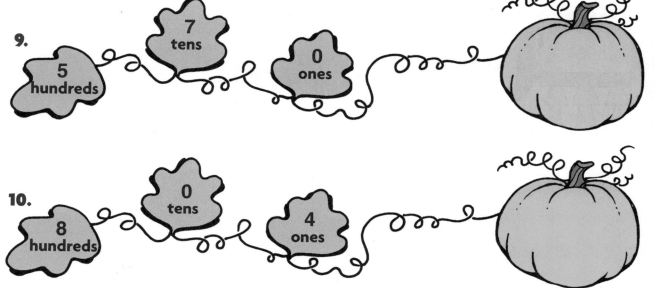

9. **5 hundreds** **7 tens** **0 ones**

10. **8 hundreds** **0 tens** **4 ones**

Regroup hundreds to tens. Remember: 1 hundred = 10 tens.

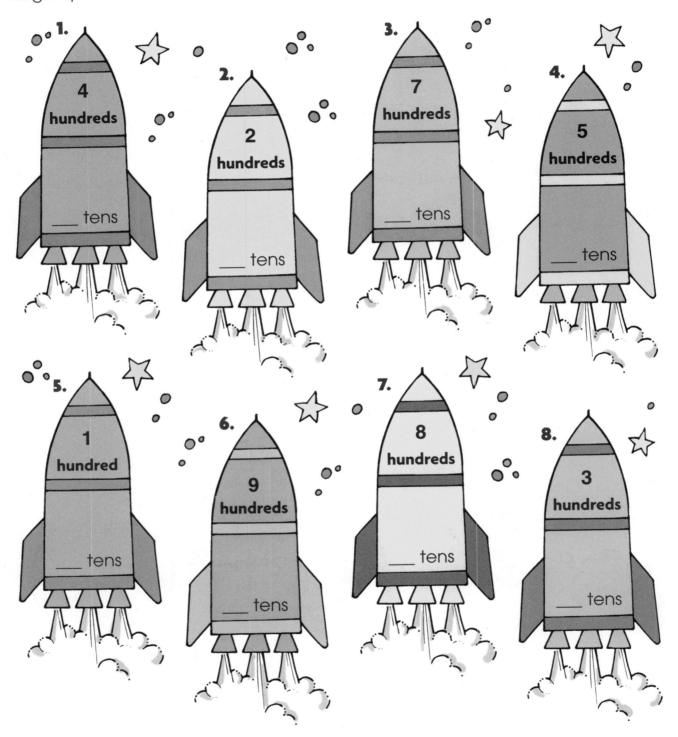

1. 4 hundreds ___ tens

2. 2 hundreds ___ tens

3. 7 hundreds ___ tens

4. 5 hundreds ___ tens

5. 1 hundred ___ tens

6. 9 hundreds ___ tens

7. 8 hundreds ___ tens

8. 3 hundreds ___ tens

Do the problems below. Then find your answers hidden in the carnival scene and circle them. Can you find all twelve answers?

15 33 + 27	27 23 + 12	34 23 + 24	15 25 + 10	16 14 + 14	12 31 + 17

28 22 + 45	43 27 + 27	10 17 + 18	29 13 + 16	37 31 + 17	51 23 + 17

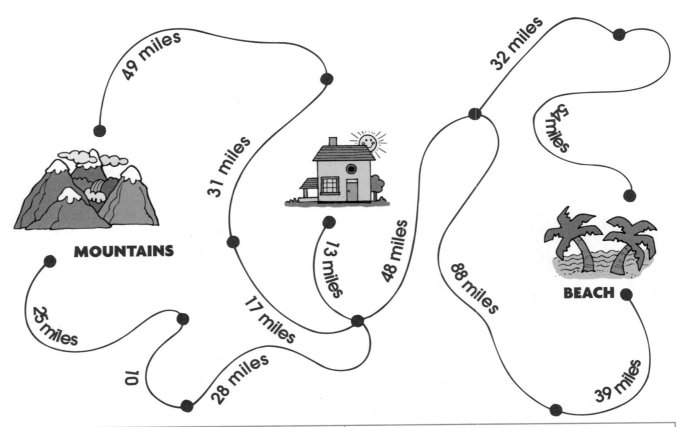

49 miles

31 miles

13 miles

17 miles

25 miles

10

28 miles

48 miles

88 miles

32 miles

45 miles

39 miles

MOUNTAINS

BEACH

A. Add the distance of each route from the house to the beach.

Route #1   Route #2

_____   _____

_____   _____

_____   _____

+ _____   + _____

_____   _____

miles   miles

B. Add the distance of each route from the house to the mountains.

Route #1   Route #2

_____   _____

_____   _____

_____   _____

+ _____   + _____

_____   _____

miles   miles

Scholastic

Sandy and Mandy are having a twin party. There are six sets of twins, but only one set of identical twins. To find the identical twins, solve the addition problems under each person. The identical twins have the same answer.

207
+ 544

126
+ 89

328
+ 348

257
+ 458

547
+ 129

624
+ 127

108
+ 107

229
+ 418

258
+ 268

379
+ 336

417
+ 109

153
+ 494

Scholastic

Add. Then trace the mole's path to the top. The mole must travel through tunnels with a zero in the sum.

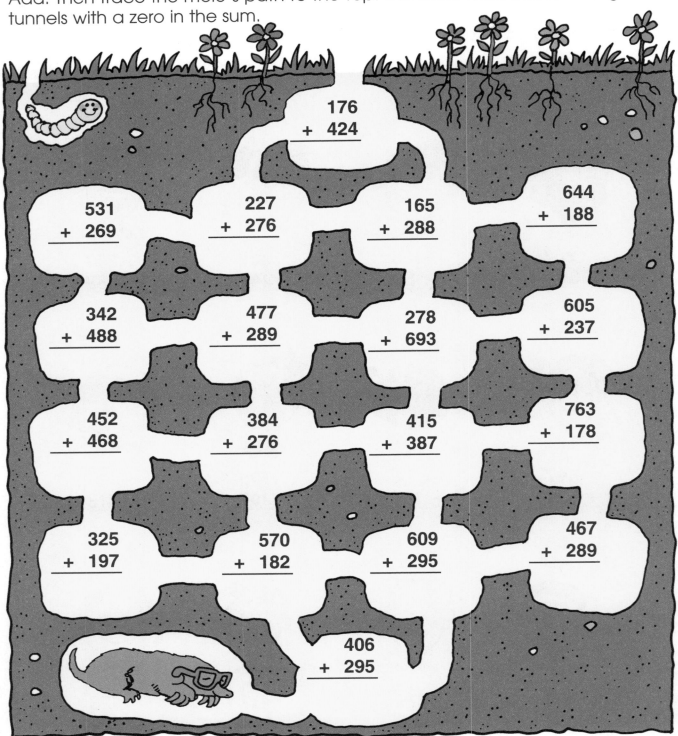

176
+ 424

531
+ 269

227
+ 276

165
+ 288

644
+ 188

342
+ 488

477
+ 289

278
+ 693

605
+ 237

452
+ 468

384
+ 276

415
+ 387

763
+ 178

325
+ 197

570
+ 182

609
+ 295

467
+ 289

406
+ 295

Scholastic

 On another piece of paper, write three more problems that have a zero in the sum.

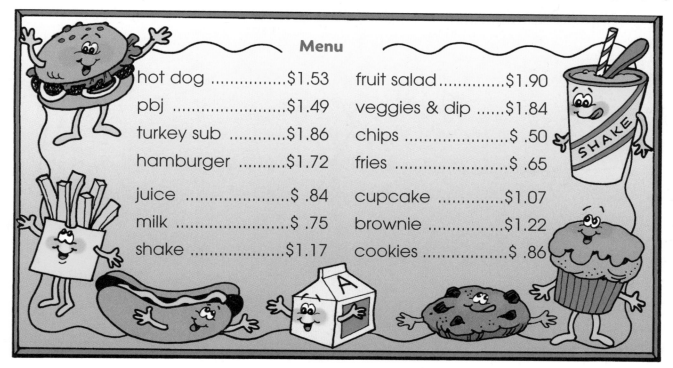

Menu

hot dog $1.53	fruit salad..............$1.90
pbj $1.49	veggies & dip $1.84
turkey sub $1.86	chips ....$ .50
hamburger $1.72	fries ....$ .65
juice ....$ .84	cupcake $1.07
milk ....$ .75	brownie $1.22
shake $1.17	cookies ....$ .86

Add.

A.

pbj

chips

milk

brownie   + _____

B.

hamburger

fries

shake   + _____

C.

turkey sub

veggies & dip

juice

cupcake   + _____

D.

hot dog

fruit salad

brownie

juice   + _____

E.

turkey sub

chips

shake   + _____

F.

pbj

cookies

milk   + _____

Add to find the perimeter of each shape.

A.

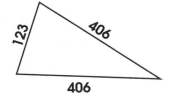

B.

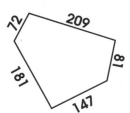

C.

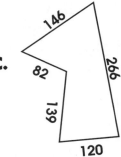

$$
\begin{array}{r}
1\,2\,3 \\
4\,0\,6 \\
+\ 4\,0\,6 \\
\hline
\end{array}
$$

+ _____

+ _____

D.

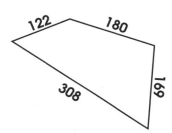

E.

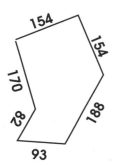

F.

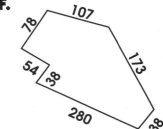

+ _____

+ _____

+ _____

Scholastic

Answer the questions.

Matthew plays the horn at different places. Last year, he played at 5 school events, 12 parties, and 7 baseball games.

1. At what type of event did Matthew play the most? _____	**2.** How many more ball games did Matthew play at than school events? _____
3. If Matthew had played at 5 more school events, how many school events would he have played at in all? _____	**4.** How many more parties did Matthew play at than baseball games? _____
5. Joe played at 10 events last year. Who played in more events, Matthew or Joe. _____	**6.** At how many different kinds of events did Matthew play? _____
7. At how many events did Matthew play in all? _____	**8.** At what type of event did Matthew play the least? _____

Scholastic

Addition Practice Test

Fill in the bubble next to the correct answer.

1.

$$\begin{array}{r} 531 \\ + 269 \\ \hline \end{array}$$

- ◯ A   800
- ◯ B   700
- ◯ C   600
- ◯ D   500

2.

$$\begin{array}{r} 609 \\ + 295 \\ \hline \end{array}$$

- ◯ F   913
- ◯ G   904
- ◯ H   813
- ◯ J   914

3.

$$\begin{array}{r} 763 \\ + 178 \\ \hline \end{array}$$

- ◯ A   832
- ◯ B   941
- ◯ C   843
- ◯ D   841

4.

$$\begin{array}{r} 176 \\ + 424 \\ \hline \end{array}$$

- ◯ F   624
- ◯ G   524
- ◯ H   500
- ◯ J   600

Scholastic

Addition Practice Test

Fill in the bubble next to the correct answer.

Jane needs 20 dollars to go camping this summer. She earned 4 dollars walking dogs. She earned 4 dollars baby-sitting. She earned 5 dollars gardening. She earned 10 dollars delivering newspapers.

5. How much money did Jane earn all together?

○ **A**   20 dollars

○ **B**   21 dollars

○ **C**   22 dollars

○ **D**   23 dollars

7. How much money did Jane earn by walking dogs and baby-sitting?

○ **A**   7 dollars

○ **B**   8 dollars

○ **C**   9 dollars

○ **D**   10 dollars

6. How much money did Jane earn by baby-sitting and gardening?

○ **F**   6 dollars

○ **G**   7 dollars

○ **H**   8 dollars

○ **J**   9 dollars

8. How much money did Jane earn delivering newspapers and gardening?

○ **F**   15 dollars

○ **G**   16 dollars

○ **H**   17 dollars

○ **J**   8 dollars

Scholastic

Subtraction

When we subtract, we take one number away from another to figure out the difference left over. Subtraction is important in our daily lives—for example, when we pay for something we need to know how much money we will get back. The activities that follow will give your child lots of practice subtracting with one and two digits.

What to Do

Have your child practice subtraction facts by doing the horizontal and vertical problems on the activity pages.

$$6 - 3 = 3$$

$$\begin{array}{r} 6 \\ -\ 3 \\ \hline 3 \end{array}$$

Some of the problems will require that your child regroup numbers. That means he or she will borrow from the number to the left. For example:

$$\begin{array}{r} ^1\cancel{2}\ ^1 5 \\ -\quad 9 \\ \hline 1\ 6 \end{array}$$

Keep On Going!

Play a subtracting game with your child. Make up subtraction problems such as: If you have 83 cards and you lose 50, how many will you have left? (33) Then have your child make up subtraction problems for you to solve.
Take turns solving subtraction problems.

Subtract. Draw petals to show the difference.

Color the bows with an even number yellow.
Color the bows with an odd number purple.

Scholastic

Subtract.

Subtract!

1. **9 – 2 =**

2. **8 – 5 =**

3. **10 – 6 =**

4. **12 – 3 =**

5. **11 – 8 =**

6. **10 – 7 =**

7. **8 – 6 =**

8. **11 – 4 =**

9. **10 – 4 =**

10. **12 – 4 =**

11. **10 – 6 =**

12. **11 – 9 =**

13. **10 – 2 =**

14. **12 – 8 =**

15. **12 – 3 =**

16. **8 – 6 =**

17. **8 – 8 =**

18. **8 – 5 =**

19. **12 – 2 =**

20. **9 – 3 =**

Subtract.

1. 7
   − 4

2. 11
   − 9

3. 8
   − 5

4. 14
   − 8

5. 9
   − 4

6. 10
   − 9

7. 12
   − 7

8. 13
   − 5

9. 13
   − 9

10. 11
    − 2

11. 13
    − 8

12. 12
    − 5

13. 10
    − 1

14. 12
    − 6

15. 11
    − 8

16. 5
    − 4

17. 11
    − 6

18. 7
    − 2

19. 9
    − 3

20. 12
    − 3

Subtract.

1. 13
    − 3

2. 16
    − 7

3. 14
    − 8

4. 15
    − 7

Subtract!

5. 10
    − 1

6. 12
    − 3

7. 16
    − 2

8. 17
    − 9

9. 11
    − 5

10. 13
    − 8

11. 15
    − 6

12. 14
    − 6

13. 15
    − 9

14. 11
    − 8

15. 13
    − 7

16. 12
    − 6

17. 10
    − 9

18. 18
    − 9

19. 11
    − 4

20. 11
    − 2

Scholastic

Subtract.

Subtract!

1. 16
    − 9

2. 17
    − 8

3. 15
    − 6

4. 13
    − 8

5. 13
    − 6

6. 13
    − 9

7. 14
    − 9

8. 18
    − 9

9. 12
    − 6

10. 10
     − 3

11. 12
     − 9

12. 15
     − 9

13. 15
     − 8

14. 11
     − 9

15. 18
     − 8

16. 16
     − 7

17. 12
     − 3

18. 14
     − 6

19. 11
     − 7

20. 10
     − 2

1. Solve the problems.

2. Find each number pair on the graph. Make a dot for each.

3. Connect the dots in the order that you make them.

4. What picture did you make?

_____

	Across	Up
1.	10 – 7 = _____	10 – 8 = _____
2.	4 – 2 = _____	3 – 1 = _____
3.	7 – 5 = _____	1 – 0 = _____
4.	8 – 0 = _____	1 – 0 = _____
5.	9 – 1 = _____	8 – 6 = _____
6.	10 – 3 = _____	7 – 5 = _____
7.	10 – 2 = _____	8 – 2 = _____
8.	8 – 3 = _____	10 – 0 = _____
9.	9 – 7 = _____	7 – 1 = _____
10.	4 – 1 = _____	5 – 3 = _____
11.	9 – 2 = _____	6 – 4 = _____

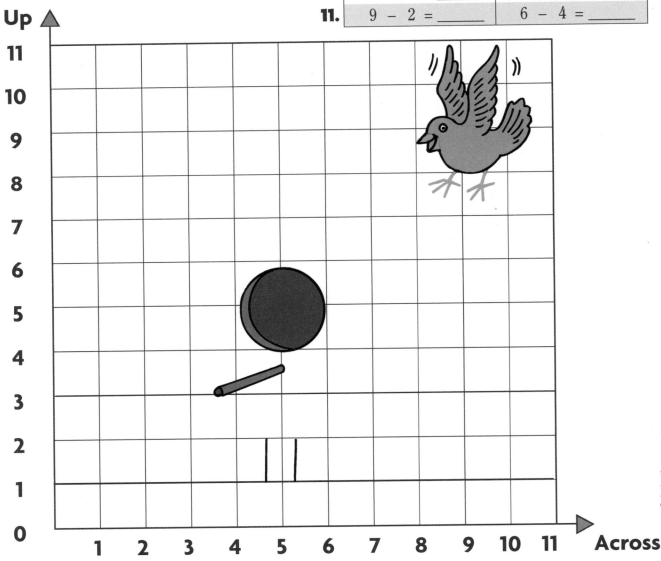

Up

11 10 9 8 7 6 5 4 3 2 1 0

1 2 3 4 5 6 7 8 9 10 11 Across

Scholastic

Do the subtraction problems. Help Mr. Squirrel find his way to the tree where he is storing acorns for the winter. Make sure he doesn't cross any odd answers.

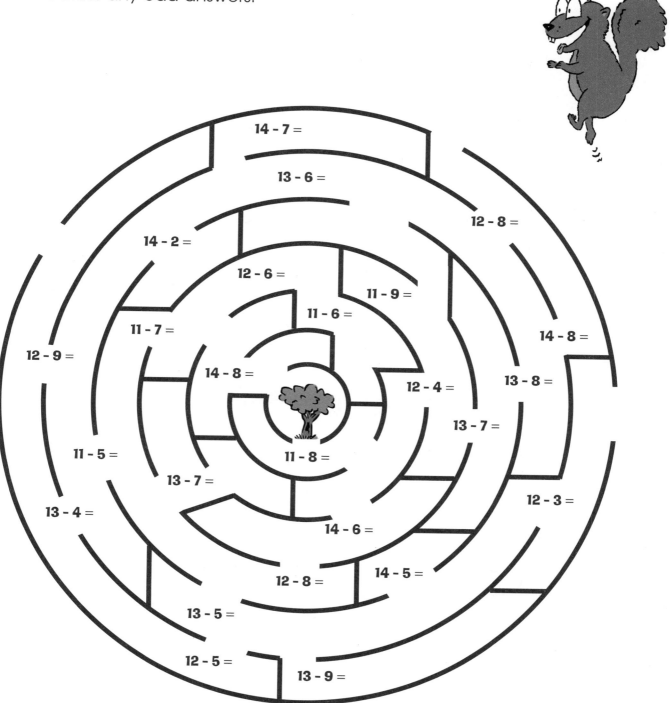

Scholastic

Subtract.

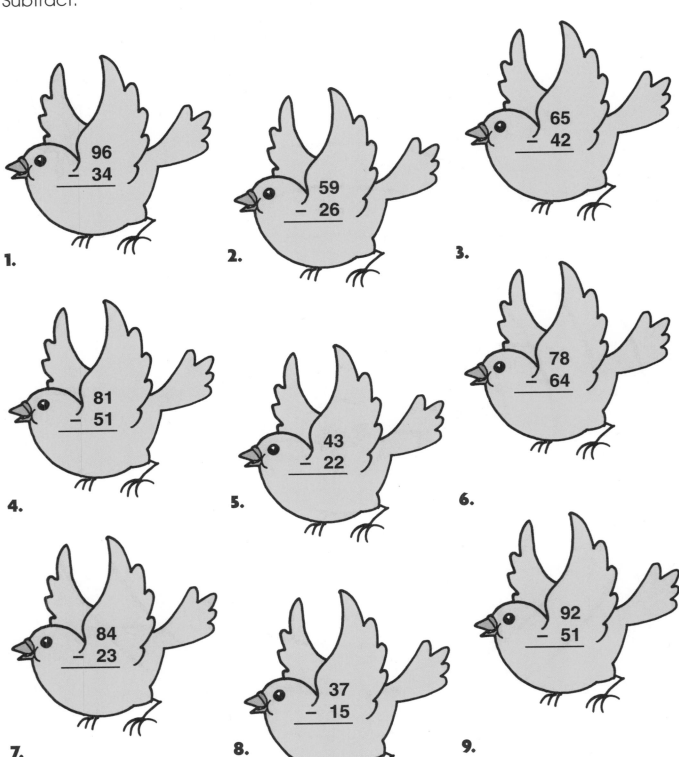

1.
$$\begin{array}{r} 96 \\ -\ 34 \\ \hline \end{array}$$

2.
$$\begin{array}{r} 59 \\ -\ 26 \\ \hline \end{array}$$

3.
$$\begin{array}{r} 65 \\ -\ 42 \\ \hline \end{array}$$

4.
$$\begin{array}{r} 81 \\ -\ 51 \\ \hline \end{array}$$

5.
$$\begin{array}{r} 43 \\ -\ 22 \\ \hline \end{array}$$

6.
$$\begin{array}{r} 78 \\ -\ 64 \\ \hline \end{array}$$

7.
$$\begin{array}{r} 84 \\ -\ 23 \\ \hline \end{array}$$

8.
$$\begin{array}{r} 37 \\ -\ 15 \\ \hline \end{array}$$

9.
$$\begin{array}{r} 92 \\ -\ 51 \\ \hline \end{array}$$

Scholastic

Subtract. Using the difference in each rain drop, write the weather words in order of their differences from least to greatest by the umbrella handle. Then color your favorite kind of "weather drop" blue.

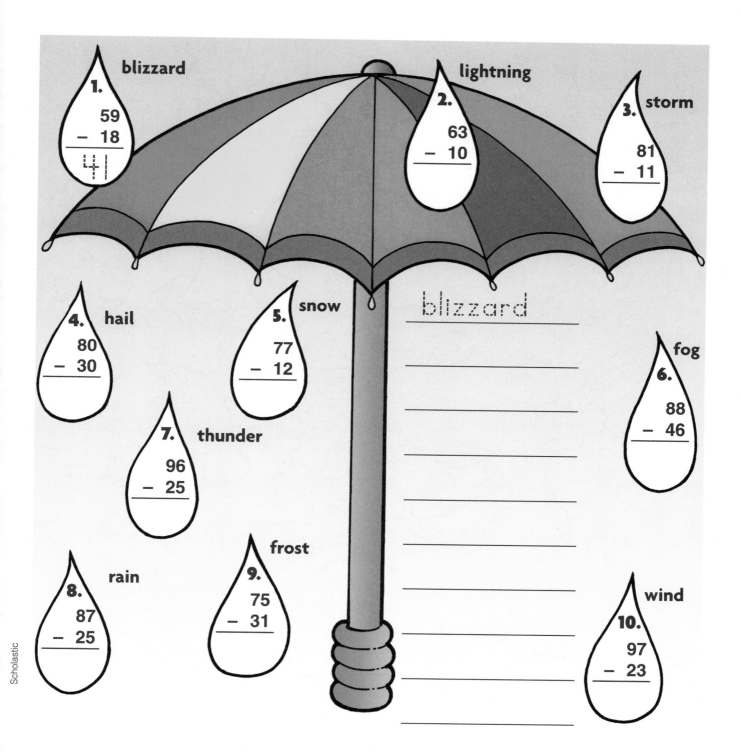

blizzard

1.

$$\begin{array}{r} 59 \\ - \ 18 \\ \hline 41 \end{array}$$

lightning

2.

$$\begin{array}{r} 63 \\ - \ 10 \\ \hline \end{array}$$

storm

3.

$$\begin{array}{r} 81 \\ - \ 11 \\ \hline \end{array}$$

hail

4.

$$\begin{array}{r} 80 \\ - \ 30 \\ \hline \end{array}$$

snow

5.

$$\begin{array}{r} 77 \\ - \ 12 \\ \hline \end{array}$$

blizzard

fog

6.

$$\begin{array}{r} 88 \\ - \ 46 \\ \hline \end{array}$$

thunder

7.

$$\begin{array}{r} 96 \\ - \ 25 \\ \hline \end{array}$$

frost

9.

$$\begin{array}{r} 75 \\ - \ 31 \\ \hline \end{array}$$

rain

8.

$$\begin{array}{r} 87 \\ - \ 25 \\ \hline \end{array}$$

wind

10.

$$\begin{array}{r} 97 \\ - \ 23 \\ \hline \end{array}$$

Subtract.

$$\begin{array}{r} 96 \\ -\ 42 \\ \hline \end{array}$$

$$\begin{array}{r} 97 \\ -\ 12 \\ \hline \end{array}$$

$$\begin{array}{r} 86 \\ -\ 43 \\ \hline \end{array}$$

$$\begin{array}{r} 99 \\ -\ 14 \\ \hline \end{array}$$

$$\begin{array}{r} 98 \\ -\ 55 \\ \hline \end{array}$$

$$\begin{array}{r} 78 \\ -\ 24 \\ \hline \end{array}$$

$$\begin{array}{r} 89 \\ -\ 22 \\ \hline \end{array}$$

$$\begin{array}{r} 77 \\ -\ 34 \\ \hline \end{array}$$

$$\begin{array}{r} 78 \\ -\ 11 \\ \hline \end{array}$$

$$\begin{array}{r} 95 \\ -\ 63 \\ \hline \end{array}$$

$$\begin{array}{r} 88 \\ -\ 56 \\ \hline \end{array}$$

Color the animals using the color code.

red	blue	purple	yellow	green
32	43	54	67	85

Scholastic

Subtract.

Subtract!

1. 63
  − 20

2. 77
  − 34

3. 62
  − 60

4. 57
  − 42

5. 38
  − 17

6. 77
  − 11

7. 54
  − 51

8. 78
  − 36

9. 43
  − 10

10. 80
  − 30

11. 68
  − 35

12. 59
  − 42

13. 72
  − 42

14. 75
  − 42

15. 58
  − 46

16. 79
  − 35

17. 87
  − 45

18. 25
  − 12

19. 46
  − 12

20. 79
  − 46

Scholastic

Subtract.

Subtract!

1.   46
   − 21

2.   38
   − 15

3.   47
   − 35

4.   66
   − 45

5.   98
   − 56

6.   87
   − 37

7.   88
   − 44

8.   36
   − 25

9.   99
   − 17

10.   68
   − 42

11.   15
   − 10

12.   83
   − 52

13.   69
   − 44

14.   65
   − 51

15.   43
   − 10

16.   39
   − 17

17.   53
   − 31

18.   78
   − 35

19.   85
   − 42

20.   80
   − 70

Scholastic

Solve the problems. If the answer is between 1 and 20, color the shape red. If
the answer is between 21 and 40, color the shape white. If the answer is
between 41 and 90, color the shape blue. Taking It Further: Write five
subtraction problems that have answers between 10 and 20.

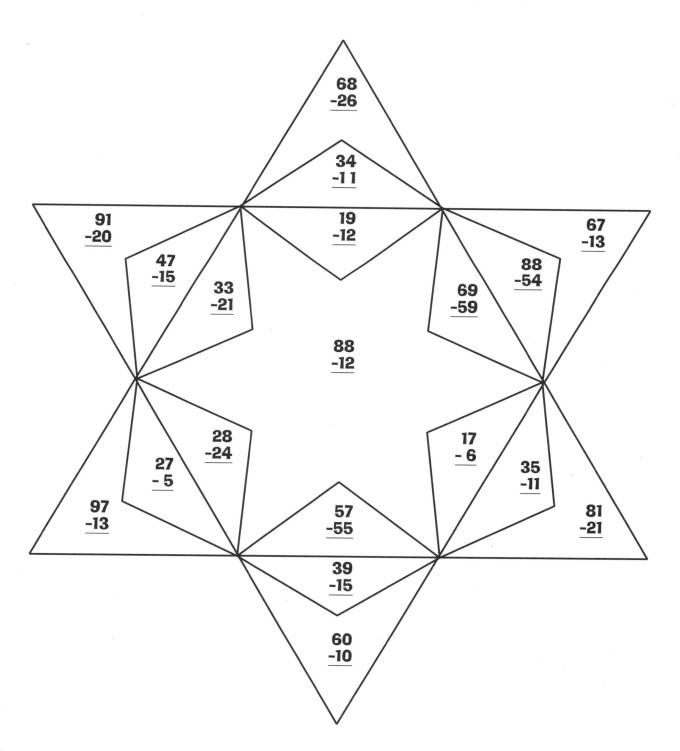

Subtract. Follow the even sums to guide the settlers to their new home.

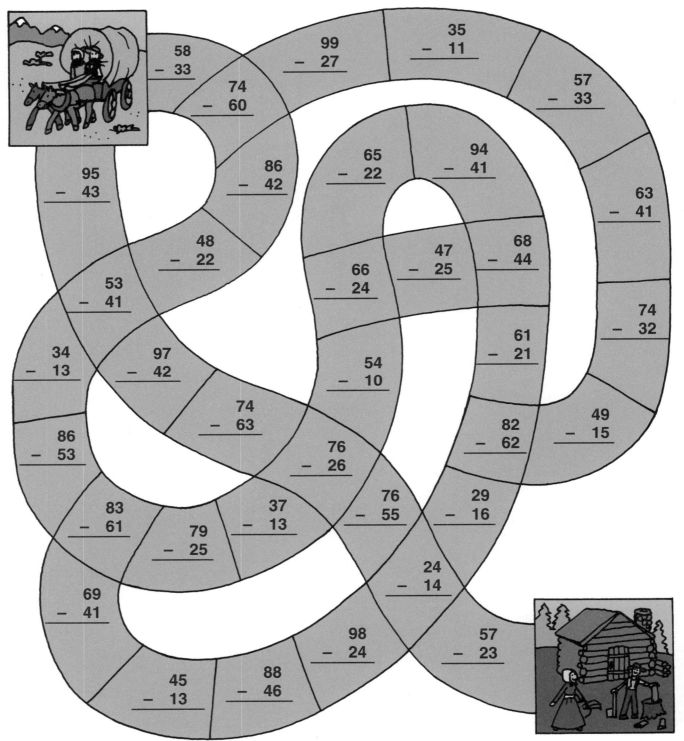

58
− 33

99
− 27

35
− 11

74
− 60

57
33

86
− 42

65
− 22

94
41

63
− 41

95
− 43

48
− 22

66
− 24

47
− 25

68
− 44

53
− 41

61
− 21

74
− 32

34
− 13

97
− 42

54
− 10

86
− 53

74
− 63

82
− 62

49
− 15

76
− 26

83
− 61

79
− 25

37
− 13

76
− 55

29
− 16

69
− 41

24
− 14

45
− 13

88
− 46

98
− 24

57
− 23

Scholastic

Subtract. Add to check.

1.

$$\begin{array}{r} 65 \\ -\ 27 \\ \hline 38 \end{array}$$

$$\begin{array}{r} 38 \\ +\ 27 \\ \hline 65 \end{array}$$

2.

$$\begin{array}{r} 77 \\ -\ 38 \\ \hline \end{array}$$

$+$ ___

3.

$$\begin{array}{r} 24 \\ -\ 15 \\ \hline \end{array}$$

$+$ ___

4.

$$\begin{array}{r} 32 \\ -\ 13 \\ \hline \end{array}$$

$+$ ___

5.

$$\begin{array}{r} 83 \\ -\ 49 \\ \hline \end{array}$$

$+$ ___

6.

$$\begin{array}{r} 50 \\ -\ 19 \\ \hline \end{array}$$

$+$ ___

7.

$$\begin{array}{r} 46 \\ -\ 29 \\ \hline \end{array}$$

$+$ ___

8.

$$\begin{array}{r} 62 \\ -\ 15 \\ \hline \end{array}$$

$+$ ___

Solve the problems. If the answer is between 1 and 50, color the shape red.
If the answer is between 51 and 100, color the shape blue. Finish the design
by coloring the other shapes with the colors of your choice.

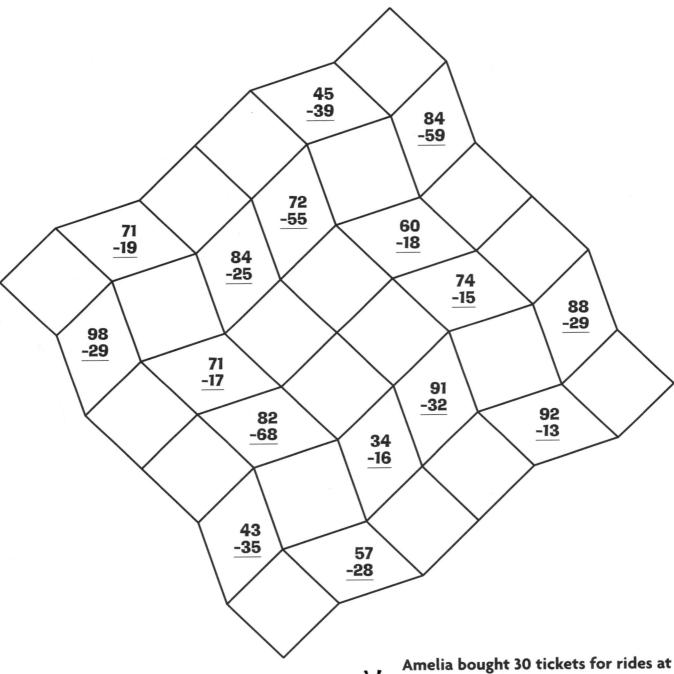

Amelia bought 30 tickets for rides at
the carnival. She used 15 tickets in
the first hour. How many tickets did
she have left? _____

Subtract. Then number the pictures in order from least to greatest.

A.

$$\begin{array}{r} 64 \\ -\ 45 \\ \hline \end{array}$$ $$\begin{array}{r} 58 \\ -\ 19 \\ \hline \end{array}$$ $$\begin{array}{r} 83 \\ -\ 46 \\ \hline \end{array}$$

B.

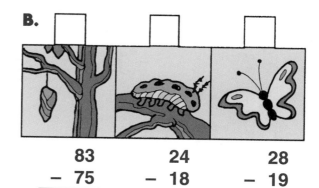

$$\begin{array}{r} 83 \\ -\ 75 \\ \hline \end{array}$$ $$\begin{array}{r} 24 \\ -\ 18 \\ \hline \end{array}$$ $$\begin{array}{r} 28 \\ -\ 19 \\ \hline \end{array}$$

C.

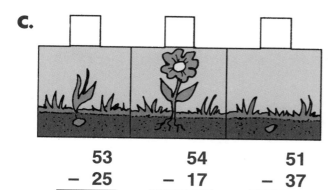

$$\begin{array}{r} 53 \\ -\ 25 \\ \hline \end{array}$$ $$\begin{array}{r} 54 \\ -\ 17 \\ \hline \end{array}$$ $$\begin{array}{r} 51 \\ -\ 37 \\ \hline \end{array}$$

D.

$$\begin{array}{r} 88 \\ -\ 59 \\ \hline \end{array}$$ $$\begin{array}{r} 91 \\ -\ 53 \\ \hline \end{array}$$ $$\begin{array}{r} 82 \\ -\ 45 \\ \hline \end{array}$$

E.

$$\begin{array}{r} 73 \\ -\ 44 \\ \hline \end{array}$$ $$\begin{array}{r} 71 \\ -\ 35 \\ \hline \end{array}$$ $$\begin{array}{r} 76 \\ -\ 28 \\ \hline \end{array}$$

F.

$$\begin{array}{r} 82 \\ -\ 64 \\ \hline \end{array}$$ $$\begin{array}{r} 34 \\ -\ 19 \\ \hline \end{array}$$ $$\begin{array}{r} 57 \\ -\ 38 \\ \hline \end{array}$$

Scholastic

Subtract.

1. 34
  − 25

2. 87
  − 19

3. 45
  − 38

4. 78
  − 29

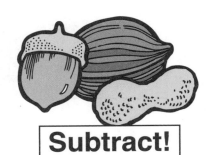

Subtract!

5. 87
  − 39

6. 65
  − 27

7. 65
  − 28

8. 44
  − 37

9. 68
  − 29

10. 55
  − 36

11. 78
  − 39

12. 87
  − 38

13. 92
  − 24

14. 68
  − 49

15. 48
  − 39

16. 96
  − 38

17. 65
  − 37

18. 35
  − 29

19. 75
  − 46

20. 88
  − 69

Scholastic

Subtract.

1. 40
  − 25

2. 78
  − 39

3. 65
  − 27

4. 62
  − 16

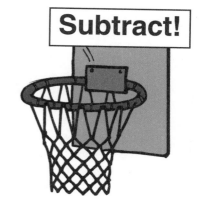
Subtract!

5. 66
  − 49

6. 25
  − 17

7. 55
  − 37

8. 42
  − 37

9. 80
  − 13

10. 53
  − 39

11. 80
  − 42

12. 86
  − 39

13. 70
  − 37

14. 87
  − 58

15. 91
  − 26

16. 45
  − 37

17. 60
  − 33

18. 98
  − 49

19. 33
  − 18

20. 63
  − 35

Scholastic

Subtract.

1. 66
− 47

2. 87
− 59

3. 86
− 28

4. 45
− 16

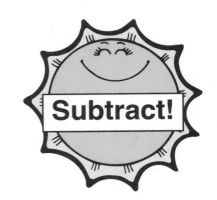

Subtract!

5. 45
− 36

6. 35
− 27

7. 77
− 58

8. 38
− 29

9. 25
− 19

10. 31
− 22

11. 87
− 69

12. 54
− 29

13. 67
− 48

14. 36
− 27

15. 48
− 29

16. 87
− 68

17. 45
− 39

18. 72
− 63

19. 58
− 49

20. 80
− 36

Scholastic

Purdy the Parakeet loves to look at herself in the mirror. Only one of these parakeets below really shows what Purdy looks like in the mirror. Can you find the right one? To check your answer, do the subtraction problems next to each bird. The answer for the correct bird is 24.

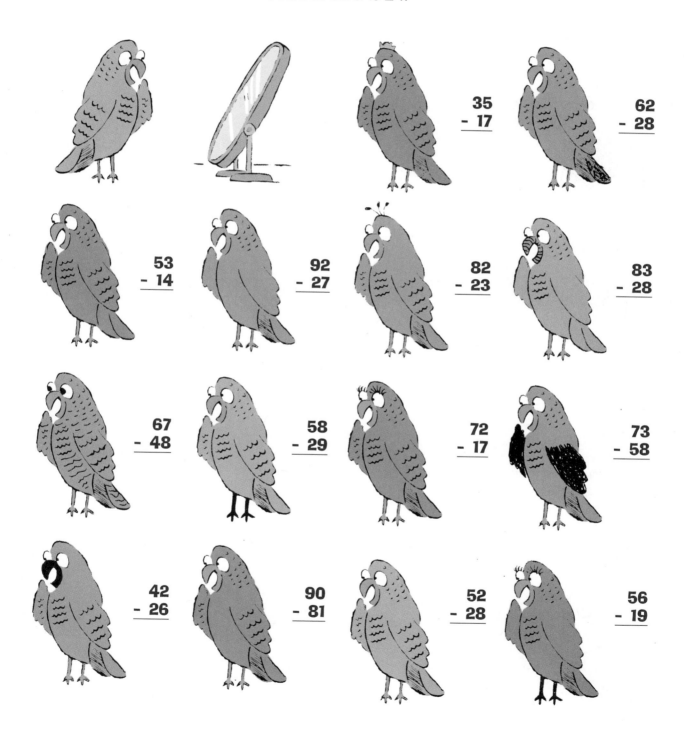

$$35 - 17$$

$$62 - 28$$

$$53 - 14$$

$$92 - 27$$

$$82 - 23$$

$$83 - 28$$

$$67 - 48$$

$$58 - 29$$

$$72 - 17$$

$$73 - 58$$

$$42 - 26$$

$$90 - 81$$

$$52 - 28$$

$$56 - 19$$

Scholastic

Draw a line to each matching difference to connect each planet to a fact about it.

Mars

$$\begin{array}{r} 694 \\ -\ 421 \\ \hline \end{array}$$

Saturn

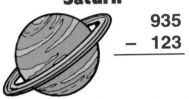

$$\begin{array}{r} 935 \\ -\ 123 \\ \hline \end{array}$$

Mercury

$$\begin{array}{r} 573 \\ -\ 241 \\ \hline \end{array}$$

Pluto

$$\begin{array}{r} 937 \\ -\ 304 \\ \hline \end{array}$$

Earth

$$\begin{array}{r} 437 \\ -\ 225 \\ \hline \end{array}$$

Uranus

$$\begin{array}{r} 968 \\ -\ 413 \\ \hline \end{array}$$

$$\begin{array}{r} 397 \\ -\ 185 \\ \hline \end{array}$$
I am a ball of rock and metal but covered with soil, rock, and water.

$$\begin{array}{r} 982 \\ -\ 650 \\ \hline \end{array}$$
I am a bare, rocky ball similar to Earth's moon.

$$\begin{array}{r} 847 \\ -\ 214 \\ \hline \end{array}$$
I am usually the farthest planet from the sun.

$$\begin{array}{r} 963 \\ -\ 151 \\ \hline \end{array}$$
I am surrounded by seven flat rings made of pieces of ice.

$$\begin{array}{r} 857 \\ -\ 302 \\ \hline \end{array}$$
I am a planet with 15 moons.

$$\begin{array}{r} 596 \\ -\ 323 \\ \hline \end{array}$$
I am called the Red Planet.

Scholastic

Draw a line to each matching difference to connect each planet or space object to a fact about it.

Venus

713
− 171
_____

Neptune

833
− 117
_____

Jupiter

675
− 216
_____

Moon

407
− 223
_____

Comet

514
− 126
_____

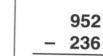

952
− 236
_____
I am a planet with days lasting only 16 hours.

857
− 469
_____
I am like a dirty snowball made of dust, ice, and gases.

612
− 428
_____
I am covered with craters.

931
− 389
_____
I am sizzling hot with no water.

892
− 433
_____
I am a giant planet with a red spot.

Complete each pattern. Then tell someone the pattern for each set of numbers.

900, 800, 700, _____, _____, _____, _____, _____, _____

900, 700, 500, _____, _____

800, 600, 400, _____

Subtract.

190
− 124

360
− 318

480
− 136

720
− 517

502
− 289

208
− 129

904
− 435

500
− 247

490
− 256

800
− 643

305
− 176

300
− 134

700
− 391

Subtraction Practice Test

Fill in the bubble next to the correct answer.

1. How many more students voted for cheese than veggie pizza?

○ **A**   15

○ **B**   16

○ **C**   17

○ **D**   18

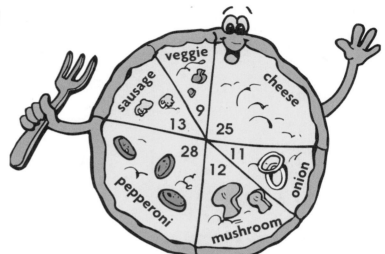

2. How many more students voted for pepperoni than sausage pizza?

○ **F**   15

○ **G**   16

○ **H**   17

○ **J**   18

3. How many more students voted for mushroom than onion pizza?

○ **A**   1

○ **B**   2

○ **C**   3

○ **D**   4

Subtraction Practice Test

Fill in the bubble next to the correct answer.

4.
$$\begin{array}{r} 51 \\ -27 \\ \hline \end{array}$$

○ A   21

○ B   23

○ C   24

○ D   25

5.
$$\begin{array}{r} 74 \\ -15 \\ \hline \end{array}$$

○ F   56

○ G   57

○ H   58

○ J   59

6.
$$\begin{array}{r} 903 \\ -189 \\ \hline \end{array}$$

○ A   614

○ B   714

○ C   19

○ D   814

7.
$$\begin{array}{r} 513 \\ -396 \\ \hline \end{array}$$

○ F   117

○ G   113

○ H   124

○ J   127

Scholastic

Multiplication

When you multiply, you add a number to itself a number of times. For example: 2 + 2 + 2 + 2 + 2 = 10 or 2 x 5 = 10. Multiplying is a quick way to add things up. The activities in this section will introduce your child to some basic multiplication facts.

What to Do

Have your child solve the vertical and horizontal multiplication problems on the activity pages. Some of the problems will require that your child carry over a number from one column to the column on the left.

On the activity pages your child is asked to color each page according to the answers to the problems. Doing so will uncover a beautiful quilt design.

Keep On Going!

Encourage your child to climb the multiplication mountain. Have him or her practice the multiplication table from 1 to 10. Then you and your child can make up problems for each other to solve.

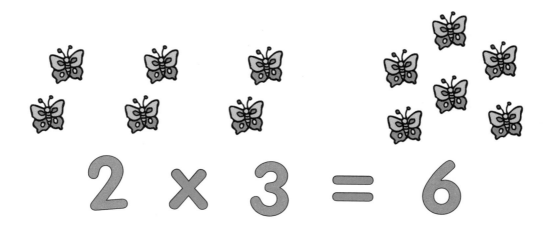

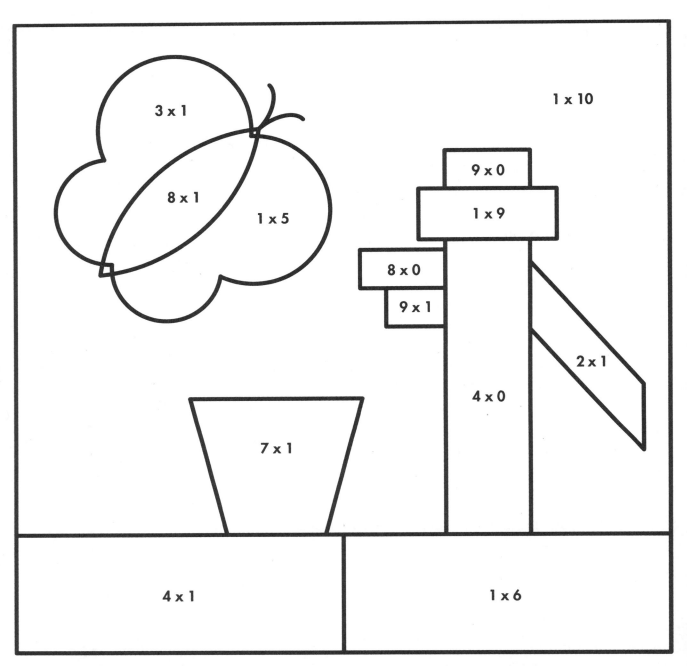

Color:
- 0 and 2 = red
- 1, 3, and 5 = orange
- 4 and 6 = green
- 7 and 8 = yellow
- 9 = black
- 10 = blue

There was a time in the history of our country when people got their water from a town pump.

Scholastic

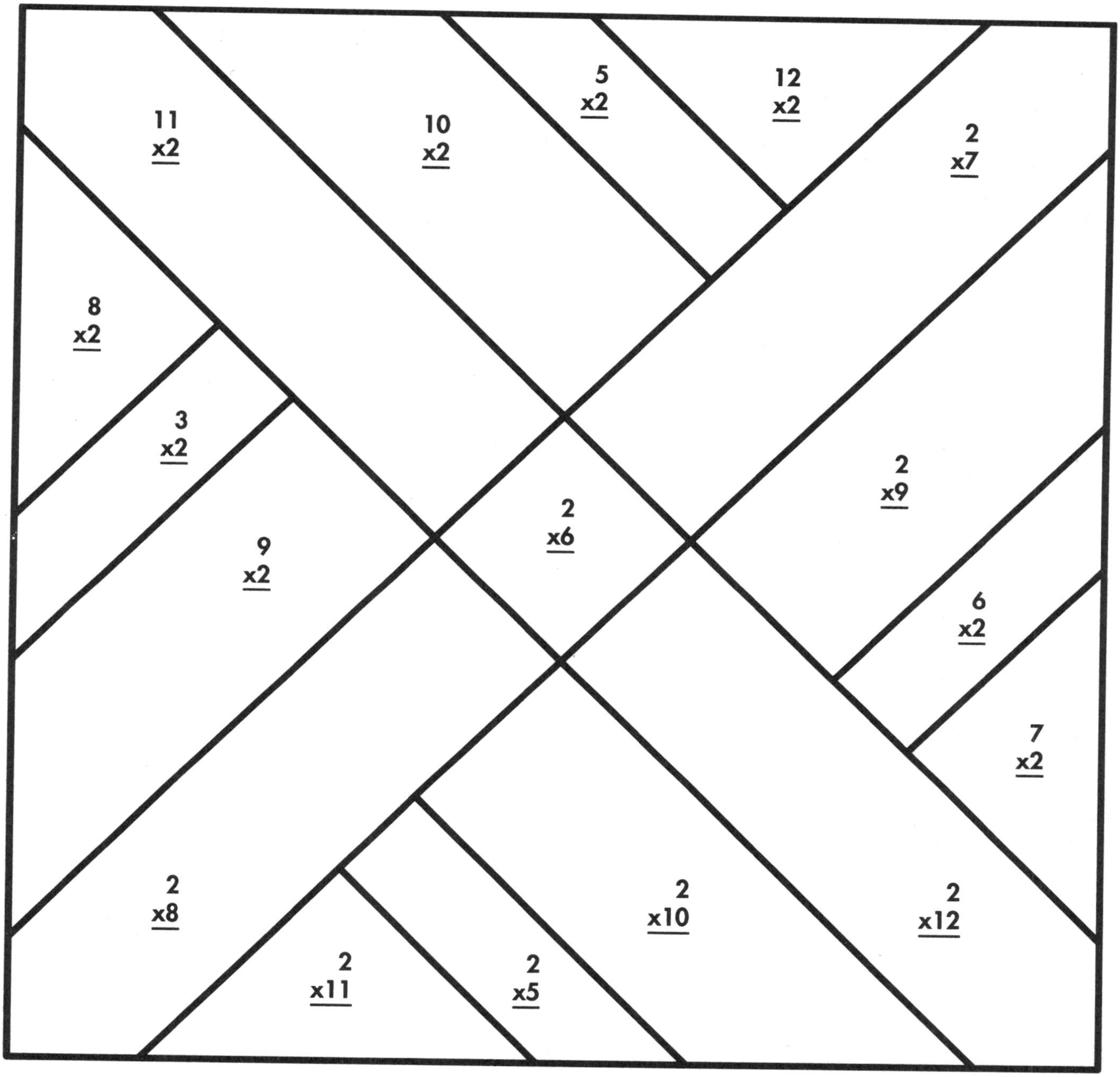

11×2

10×2

5×2

12×2

2×7

8×2

3×2

2×9

9×2

2×6

6×2

7×2

2×8

2×10

2×12

2×11

2×5

Color:
  6, 8, 10, and 12 = red
          14 and 16 = purple
          18 and 20 = yellow
          22 and 24 = green

A young girl named this design after her mother, Mary Tenney Gray.

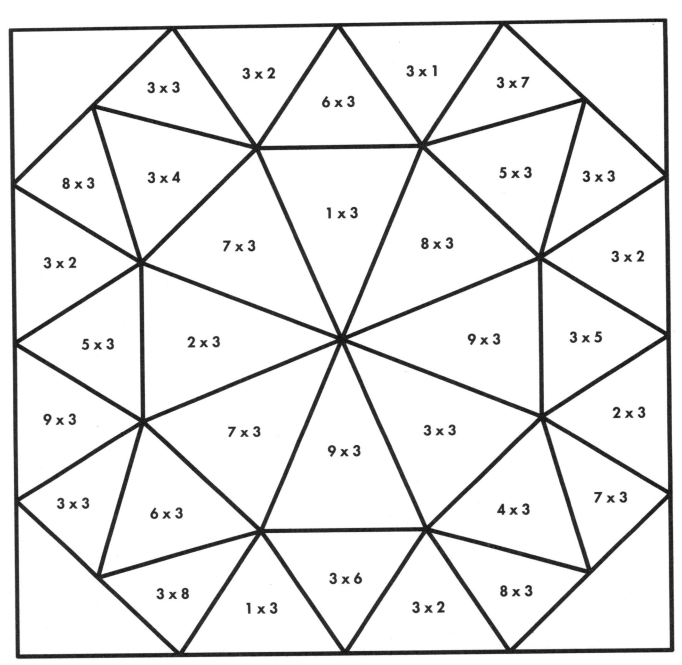

Color:
- 3, 6, and 27 = red
- 12, 15, and 18 = orange
- 9, 21, and 24 = green

After you color this design, you'll see the shape of the morning star.

Scholastic

4 x 4

10 x 4

4 x 0

6 x 4

4 x 4

11 x 4

4 x 3

3 x 4

7 x 4

9 x 4

8 x 4

1 x 4

4 x 5

4 x 2

4 x 9

4 x 6

4 x 8

5 x 4

4 x 4

4 x 8

2 x 4

3 x 4

4 x 10

4 x 7

4 x 5

Color:

0, 4, and 8 = brown

24, 28, 32, 36, 40, and 44 = blue

12, 16, and 20 = red

This design has the shape of the windmills in Holland.

Scholastic

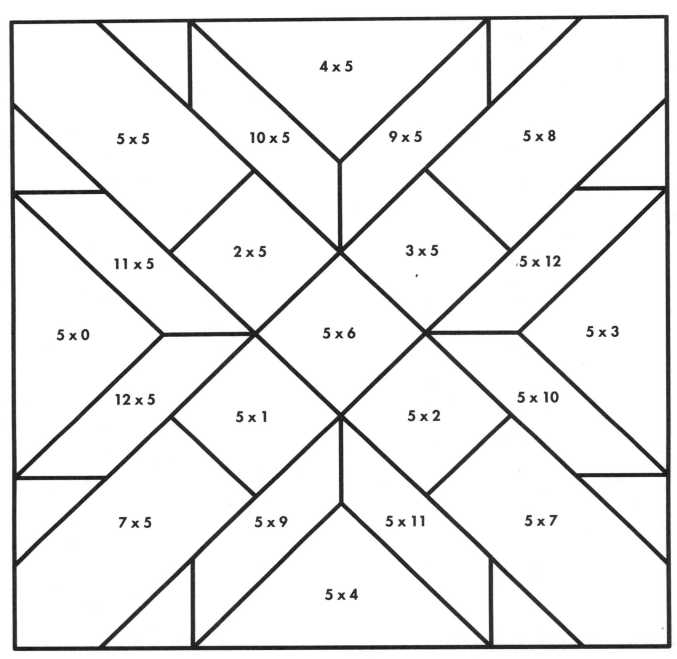

4 x 5

5 x 5   10 x 5   9 x 5   5 x 8

11 x 5   2 x 5   3 x 5   5 x 12

5 x 0   5 x 6   5 x 3

12 x 5   5 x 1   5 x 2   5 x 10

7 x 5   5 x 9   5 x 11   5 x 7

5 x 4

**If the answer is between
0 and 20, color the space yellow.**

**If the answer is between
25 and 40, color the space orange.**

**This pattern is named for a direction
in square dancing.**

**If the answer is between
45 and 60, color the space green.**

Scholastic

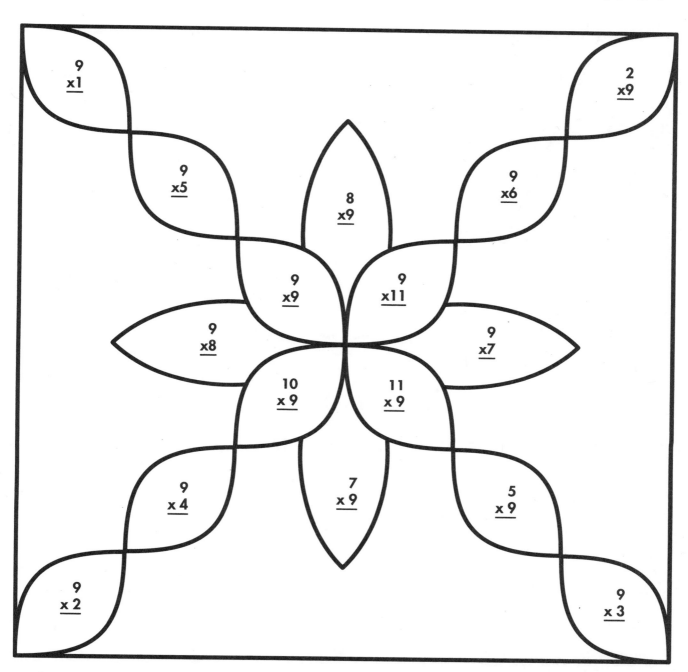

Color:

    9, 18, and 27 = blue
        63 and 72 = green
    36, 45, and 54 = yellow
    81, 90, and 99 = red

In pioneer days, people made their own beads out of wood or glass. Then they strung them into necklaces.

Scholastic

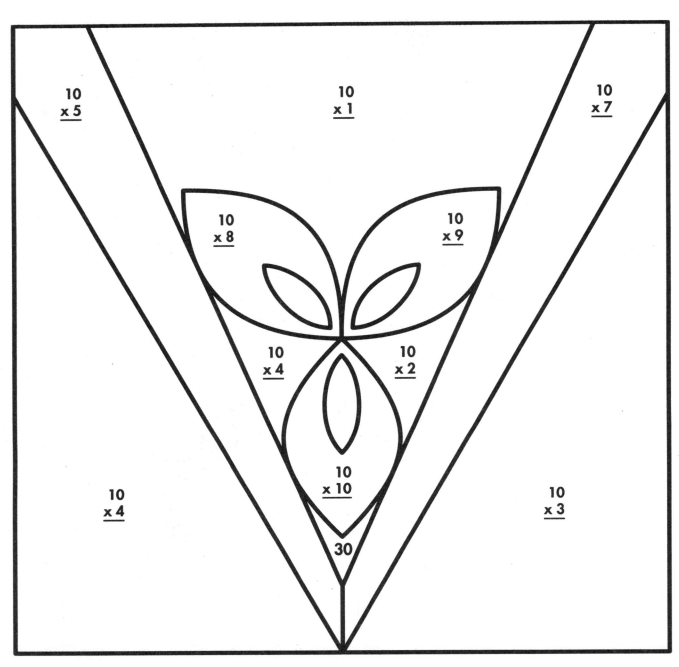

If the answer is from
10 to 40, color the space brown.
If the answer is from
50 to 70, color the space green.

When you solve the color code for
this pattern, you may see why it
has its name.

_____

If the answer is from
80 to 100, color the space blue.

Scholastic

Multiplication Practice Test

Fill in the bubble next to the correct answer.

1. $9 \times 6 =$

    ○ **A**   45

    ○ **B**   54

    ○ **C**   63

    ○ **D**   52

2. $4 \times 5 =$

    ○ **F**   20

    ○ **G**   9

    ○ **H**   15

    ○ **J**   1

3.
$$\begin{array}{r} 2 \\ \times\ 7 \\ \hline \end{array}$$

    ○ **A**   9

    ○ **B**   5

    ○ **C**   14

    ○ **D**   27

4.
$$\begin{array}{r} 3 \\ \times\ 6 \\ \hline \end{array}$$

    ○ **F**   6

    ○ **G**   0

    ○ **H**   10

    ○ **J**   9

Scholastic

Multiplication Practice Test

Choose a sticker to place here.

Fill in the bubble next to the correct answer.

5. 6 x 5 =

- ○ A   26
- ○ B   30
- ○ C   40
- ○ D   60

6.
$$\begin{array}{r} 3 \\ \times\ 7 \\ \hline \end{array}$$

- ○ F   17
- ○ G   21
- ○ H   10
- ○ J   11

7.
$$\begin{array}{r} 5 \\ \times\ 10 \\ \hline \end{array}$$

- ○ A   50
- ○ B   15
- ○ C   5
- ○ D   20

8.
$$\begin{array}{r} 4 \\ \times\ 4 \\ \hline \end{array}$$

- ○ F   4
- ○ G   8
- ○ H   12
- ○ J   16

Scholastic

Time, Money & Measurement

What time is it? How much does it cost? How long is that rope? These are questions your child might ask or be asked. The answers may be important to what he or she does that day. The activities in this section give your child practice with the important concepts of time, money, and measurement.

What to Do

Have your child work out the problems on each activity page. Check the answers together. For a quick check, check the answer key at the back of the book.

Keep On Going!

Play 20 questions. Make up questions concerning time, money, or measurement for your child to answer. Have him or her make up questions for you to answer. Ask questions such as: *What time is it? If you have $5.00 and buy hairclips for $1.50 and a slice of pizza for $2.50, how much money will you have left? How much taller are you than your friend Gabe?*

	Mike's Afternoon Schedule:
12:25	Eat Lunch
1:45	Go to George's House
3:15	Come Home from George's House
5:00	Take a Bath
7:00	Eat Dinner
7:45	Read a Book
8:30	Go to Bed

Write the activity that Mike has planned for each time shown below.

1.

_____

2.

_____

3.

_____

4.

_____

When the big hand points to the 3, then it is 15 minutes past the hour. If it points to the 9, it is 45 minutes past the hour.

It is 4:15.

It is 7:45.

Write the time that each clock below shows.

1.

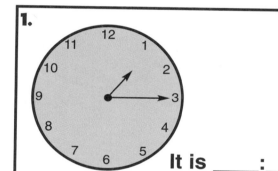

It is ____:____

2.

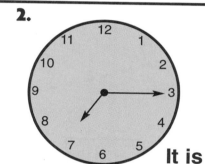

It is ____:____

3.

It is ____:____

4.

It is ____:____

5.

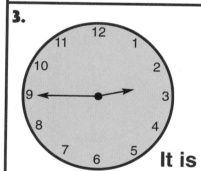

It is ____:____

6.

It is ____:____

Scholastic

Draw a line to match each time to the correct clock.

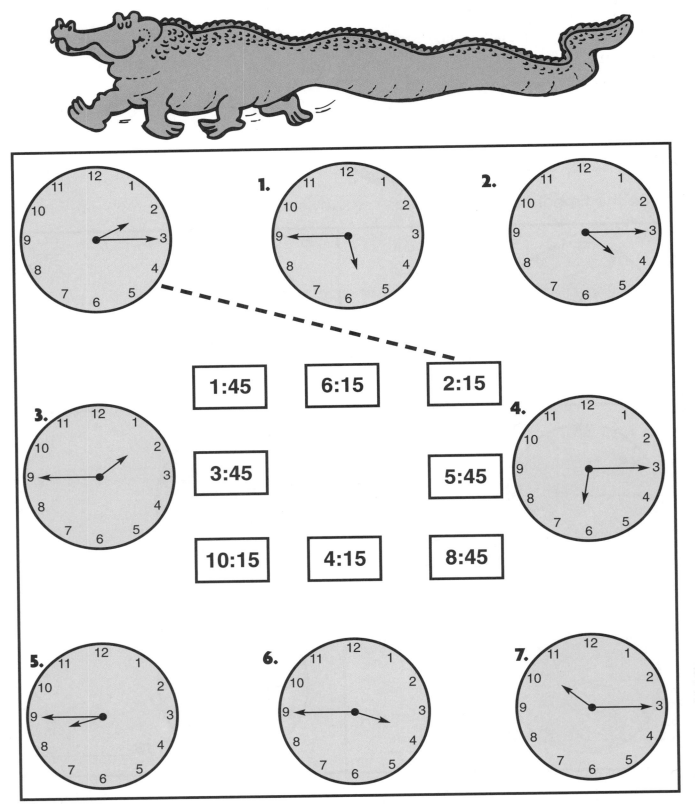

1.

2.

1:45   6:15   2:15

3.   3:45   5:45   4.

10:15   4:15   8:45

5.   6.   7.

Scholastic

Draw a circle around the correct time underneath each of the clocks.

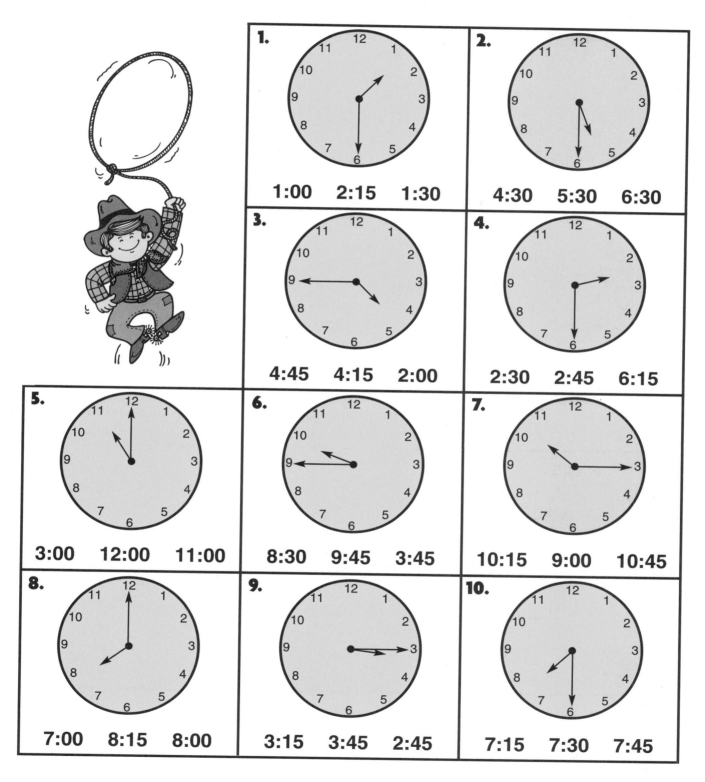

1.
1:00   2:15   1:30

2.
4:30   5:30   6:30

3.
4:45   4:15   2:00

4.
2:30   2:45   6:15

5.
3:00   12:00   11:00

6.
8:30   9:45   3:45

7.
10:15   9:00   10:45

8.
7:00   8:15   8:00

9.
3:15   3:45   2:45

10.
7:15   7:30   7:45

Add the coins and fill in the blanks.

1.

one quarter = _____ ¢

2.

two quarters = _____ ¢

3.

one half dollar = _____ ¢

Fill in the chart.

	How many quarters are needed?	How many half dollars are needed?
4. $1.00		
5. $1.50		
6. 50¢		

Scholastic

Find the value of each set of coins.

1.

       =

_____

2.

       =

_____

3.

       =

_____

4.

    =

_____

5.

       =

_____

Scholastic

Match each set of coins to the correct amount.

1.

37¢

2.

82¢

71¢

3.

62¢

4.

Scholastic

Circle the set of coins that is worth more.

1.

a.

b.

2.

a.

b.

3.

a.

b.

4.

a.

b.

Circle the coins you would need to buy each item.

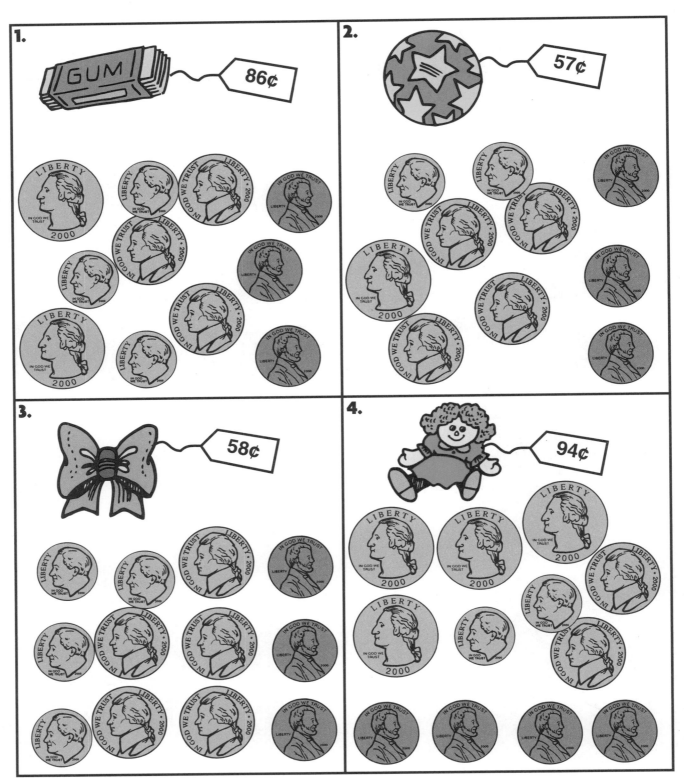

1. GUM 86¢

2. 57¢

3. 58¢

4. 94¢

Write the fewest number of coins you could use to make the amounts below.
Use the following coins in combination: quarters, nickels, dimes, and pennies.

1.   **65¢** _____

_____

2.   **97¢** _____

_____

3.   **38¢** _____

_____

4.   **74¢** _____

_____

5.   **81¢** _____

_____

6.   **56¢** _____

_____

Solve the problems.

1. Henry arrived at the park at 10:15. He flew his kite for 2 hours. What time did he stop flying his kite?	**2.** Megan is baking a cake. She put the cake in the oven at 3:02. The directions say to bake the cake for 35 minutes. What time should she take the cake out of the oven?
3. Mario rode his bike for 3 hours. If he stopped at 5:20, what time did he start?	**4.** A train left for Center City at 4:12. The train took 3 hours and fifteen minutes to get to Marksville. What time did the train arrive in Marksville?
5. The class recess starts at 1:50 and lasts for 25 minutes. What time does recess end?	**6.** Hannah went to the library yesterday. She arrived there at 9:00. She spent 2 hours reading, then spent 20 minutes riding her bike home. What time did she get home?

Scholastic

Fill in the grid below to show how many bills and coins you would need to pay the exact amount for each item.

	ten dollar bills	five dollar bills	one dollar bills	quarters	nickels	dimes	pennies
1.							
2.							
3.							
4.							
5.							
6.							

Use an inch ruler to draw a worm for each length.

> **Key**
> One inch can also
> be written as 1".

1. 4" long worm

2. 5" long worm

3. 8" long worm

4. 6" long worm

Draw an **X** on each snake that is longer than 3 inches.

5.

6.

7.

Use a ruler to measure the line segments. Write your answers in inches. Then add to find the total length.

1.

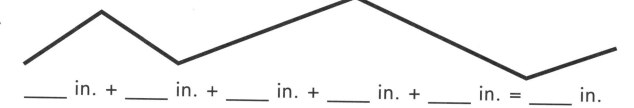

____ in. + ____ in. + ____ in. + ____ in. + ____ in. = ____ in.

2.

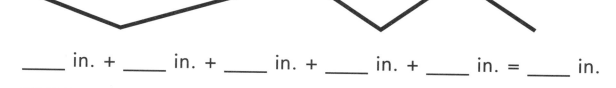

____ in. + ____ in. + ____ in. + ____ in. + ____ in. = ____ in.

3.

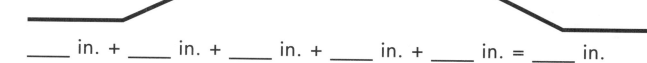

____ in. + ____ in. + ____ in. = ____ in.

4.

____ in. + ____ in. + ____ in. + ____ in. + ____ in. = ____ in.

5. Trace the longest line with a red crayon.

a. _____

b. _____

c. _____

6. Trace the shortest line with a blue crayon.

a. _____

b. _____

c. _____

7. Trace the longest line with a green crayon.

a.   b.   c.

Use the chart to find what size each person wears. Circle your answer.

1. Dale has a 28" chest. What size T-shirt does Dale wear?

Small   Medium   Large

2. Chris has a 27" waist. What size shorts does Chris wear?

Small   Medium   Large

3. Pat wears an 11" sandal. What size sandal does Pat wear?

Small   Medium   Large

4. Cam has a 24" waist. What size shorts does Cam wear?

Small   Medium   Large

5. Sam wears a 4" sandal. What size sandal does Sam wear?

Small   Medium   Large

6. Alex has a 34" chest. What size T-shirt does Alex wear?

Small   Medium   Large

Key

One inch can also be written as 1".

Beachwear-4-U Size Chart

T-Shirts
(chest size)

20"–25" Small

26"–30" Medium

31"–35" Large

Shorts
(waist size)

20"–22" Small

23"–25" Medium

36"–28" Large

Sandals
(shoe size)

4"–6" Small

7"–9" Medium

10"–12" Large

Scholastic

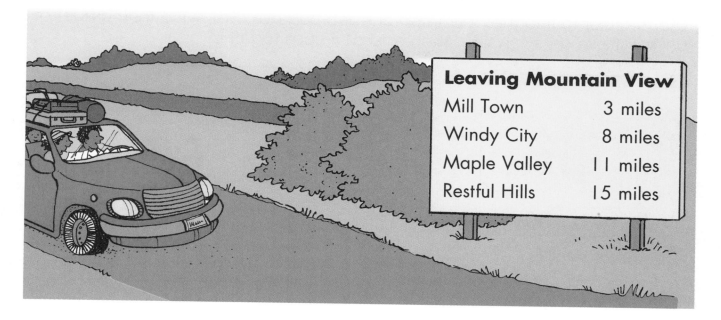

Use the sign to answer the questions.

1. Which town will the family reach next? _____

2. How far away is Mill Town? _____ miles

3. Which towns are more than 10 miles away now?

_____ and _____

4. How many miles are between Mill Town and Restful Hills?

_____ miles

5. How far is Maple Valley from Windy City? _____ miles

6. Which town is the farthest from Mountain View? _____

Use the ruler to find the perimeter for each bug box. First, write the number of units that are on each side. Then add all 4 sides together.

1.

_____ + _____ + _____ + _____

= _____ units

2.

_____ + _____ + _____ + _____

= _____ units

3.

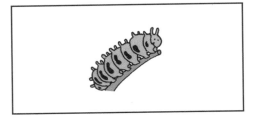

_____ + _____ + _____ + _____

= _____ units

4.

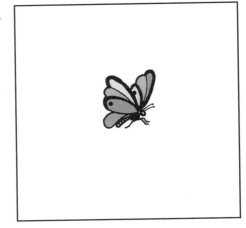

_____ + _____ + _____ + _____

= _____ units

5.  _____ + _____ + _____ + _____

= _____ units

6. _____ + _____ + _____ + _____

= _____ units

7.

_____ + _____ + _____ + _____

= _____ units

1	2	3	4	5	6	7	8	9	10

Scholastic

Estimate the length of each ribbon in centimeters (cm). Use a centimeter ruler to check your estimate. Write your answers.

Estimate   **Actual**

1.

_____ cm   _____ cm

2.

_____ cm   _____ cm

3.

_____ cm   _____ cm

4.

_____ cm   _____ cm

5.

_____ cm   _____ cm

6. The Tool Bench

Cut a 14-centimeter length of paper into three pieces. On the dots, tape the paper from shortest to longest. Measure and write the length of each piece of paper.

_____cm

_____cm

_____cm

Time, Money & Measurement Practice Test

Fill in the bubble next to the correct answer.

1. What time does the clock show?

○ **A**   9:35

○ **B**   8:35

○ **C**   8:40

○ **D**   8:20

2. What time does the clock show?

○ **F**   4:10

○ **G**   3:10

○ **H**   2:00

○ **J**   3:20

3. What time does the clock show?

○ **A**   12:05

○ **B**   12:55

○ **C**   11:55

○ **D**   3:05

4. What time does the clock show?

○ **F**   2:25

○ **G**   6:40

○ **H**   1:25

○ **J**   5:10

Scholastic

Time, Money & Measurement Practice Test

Fill in the bubble next to the correct answer.

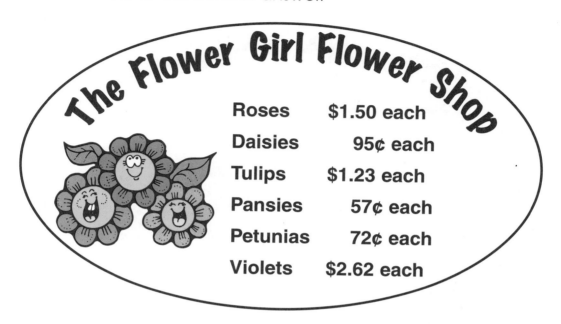

The Flower Girl Flower Shop

Roses	$1.50 each
Daisies	95¢ each
Tulips	$1.23 each
Pansies	57¢ each
Petunias	72¢ each
Violets	$2.62 each

5. How much money would you need to buy 1 rose, 2 daisies, and 2 petunias?

◯ **A** $4.84

◯ **B** $4.83

◯ **C** $3.82

◯ **D** $1.82

6. How much money would you need to buy 2 tulips, 2 violets, and 3 pansies?

◯ **F** $7.49

◯ **G** $8.43

◯ **H** $8.41

◯ **J** $9.41

Scholastic

Time, Money & Measurement Practice Test

Fill in the bubble next to the correct answer.

7. What is the distance between the Umbrella Shop and Beach Toys 4 U?

◯ **A**   5 yards

◯ **B**   6 yards

◯ **C**   7 yards

◯ **D**   10 yards

8. What is the distance between the Kite Shop and Aqua Pets?

◯ **F**   10 yards

◯ **G**   11 yards

◯ **H**   12 yards

◯ **J**   20 miles

Scholastic

Get Ready for
Grade 3

In this section of the workbook, your child will get a preview of the new skills he or she will learn in Grade 3. The activity pages in this section were chosen to help your child develop the skills necessary to be successful. Here are some of the skills and concepts covered:

• Identifying and using inflectional endings

• Identifying commonly misspelled words

• Identifying unusual spellings of vowel sounds

• Identifying letters with more than one sound and one spelling

• Identifying story elements

• Using dictionary skills

• Understanding idioms

• Understanding palindromes

• Identifying words that are often confused

• Identifying sentences and sentence fragments

• Using present-tense, past-tense, and helping verbs

• Combining sentences

• Writing sequenced paragraphs

• Understanding concepts related to multiplication

• Understanding concepts related to fractions

• Understanding concepts related to time and money

When a word ends with one vowel and one consonant (VC), double the consonant before adding an ending. For example, run *becomes* running. *When a word ends with a silent* e, *the* e *is dropped before adding an ending. For example,* rake *becomes* raking.

A. Read and write each word. Then organize the list words by their endings.

List Words

1. swimmer _____
2. wisest _____
3. hoped _____
4. shopping _____
5. clapped _____
6. safer _____
7. biggest _____
8. getting _____
9. freezer _____
10. coming _____
11. stopped _____
12. whitest _____

-er ending
_____
_____
_____

-est ending
_____
_____
_____

-ed ending
_____
_____
_____

-ing ending
_____
_____
_____

Challenge Words

13. champion _____
14. medal _____
15. compete _____

B. Write four list words that have long-vowel sounds.

_____ _____ _____ _____

Scholastic

A. Read each base word and write its matching list word with an ending. Then check the rule that applies to each word.

Base Word	List Word	Double the final consonant.	Drop the silent *e*.
1. big			
2. hope			
3. come			
4. get			
5. white			
6. wise			

B. Write a list word to complete each sentence. The shaded boxes will answer the riddle.

What did the sneezing champion win at the Olympics?

1. Are you _____ over today?
2. We are _____ for new shoes.
3. We _____ at the end of the show.
4. Our bus _____ at the corner.

5. My best friend is a strong _____.
6. Let's get ice cream from the _____.
7. I _____ my mother would agree.
8. Riding a bike is _____ with a helmet.

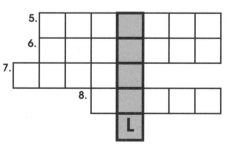

C. Find and circle the challenge words hidden in the Olympic rings. Write them on the lines.

_____

_____

_____

Scholastic

Some words do not follow common spelling patterns. Their spellings must be memorized.

A. Read and write each word. Then write an idea that will help you memorize each spelling. For example, *been* has two *e*'s.

List Words

1. been _____ _____
2. other _____ _____
3. favorite _____ _____
4. does _____ _____
5. these _____ _____
6. before _____ _____
7. friend _____ _____
8. always _____ _____
9. their _____ _____
10. done _____ _____
11. people _____ _____
12. thought _____ _____

Challenge Words

13. mammal _____
14. canines _____
15. breed _____

B. Write four list words that will be the toughest to learn to spell.

_____ _____ _____ _____

Scholastic

The /ô/ **sound** *as in* paw *can be spelled* au, aw, *or* augh.

A. Read and write each word. Then organize the list words by their ô sound spelling.

List Words

		au	*aw*
1.	hawk	_____	_____	_____
2.	daughter	_____	_____	_____
3.	awful	_____	_____	_____
4.	because	_____	_____	_____
5.	naughty	_____	_____	_____
6.	pause	_____		
7.	caught	_____	*augh*	
8.	dawn	_____	_____	
9.	sauce	_____	_____	
10.	author	_____	_____	
11.	crawl	_____	_____	
12.	taught	_____		

Challenge Words

13. food chain _____

14. producer _____

15. consumer _____

B.  Write four list words that will be tough to learn to spell.

_____ _____ _____ _____

Scholastic

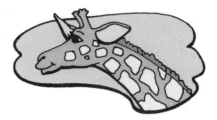

The /s/ **sound** *is sometimes spelled with the letter* c.
The /j/ **sound** *is sometimes spelled with the letter* g.

A. Read and write each word. Then organize the list words by their sounds.

 List Words

		"*c*" spellings that sound like /*s*/	"*g*" spellings that sound like /*j*/
1. giant	_____		
2. giraffe	_____		
3. office	_____	_____	_____
4. excite	_____	_____	_____
5. strange	_____	_____	_____
6. fence	_____	_____	_____
7. gentle	_____	_____	_____
8. center	_____	_____	_____
9. since	_____		
10. danger	_____		
11. large	_____		
12. price	_____		

Challenge Words

13. monkey _____

14. antelope _____

15. elephant _____

B. An adjective is a describing word. Write four list words that could be used to describe an animal.

_____ _____ _____ _____

Scholastic

A. Proofread the report. Circle the eight misspelled words. Then write them correctly on the lines below.

Our Class Trip

What a great field trip! We went to the city zoo to observe grassland animals. The most interesting was the geraff. I didn't expect such a larg animal to be so jentle. I picked a dandelion and held it over the fense toward the giraffe. It strolled over and stretched its neck to smell the senter of the flower. It must have known that there was no danjer because it wrapped its gient tongue around the dandelion and took it right out of my hand! It was such a stranje feeling! I can't wait to go back!

_____   _____   _____

_____   _____   _____

_____   _____

B. Write the list word for each definition. The shaded boxes will answer the riddle.

What do you call a giraffe's necklace?

1. big; rhymes with barge
2. a place where business occurs
3. in a kind manner
4. odd
5. something that may cause harm
6. to stir up
7. from then until now
8. cost

C. Find and circle the challenge words hidden in the maze. Write them on the lines.

_____

_____

_____

Scholastic

The Invention of the Telephone

Alexander Graham Bell invented the telephone. He was a teacher of the deaf in Boston. At night, he worked on experiments using a telegraph. Once when the metal in the telegraph stuck, Bell's assistant plucked the metal to loosen it. Bell, who was in another room, heard the sound in his receiver. He understood that the vibrations of the metal had traveled down the electric current to the receiver. He continued to work on this idea.

March 10, 1876, was the first time Alexander Graham Bell successfully spoke words over a telephone line. He was about to test a new transmitter when he spilled some battery acid on his clothes. He cried out to his assistant who was in another room, "Mr. Watson, come here! I want you!" Watson heard every word clearly on the telephone and rushed into the room.

partial page from inventor's notebook

Bell demonstrated his invention to many people. Over time, more and more telephone lines were installed, and people began to use the invention in their homes and businesses.

1. **Who invented the telephone?** _____

2. **What was his regular job?** _____

3. **What did Mr. Bell say to Mr. Watson during the first telephone conversation?**

   _____

4. **Who was Mr. Watson?** _____

5. **How did people first learn about the telephone?** _____

   _____

Scholastic

Follow the directions to play each word game.

1. A palindrome is a word that is spelled the same forward or backward. Write each word backward. Circle each word that is a palindrome. Put an X on each word that is not.

wow _____

dad _____

mom _____

funny _____

noon _____

tall _____

deed _____

2. Some words imitate the noise that they stand for. For example, when you say "pop," it sounds like a popping sound! That is called onomatopoeia. Unscramble each noise word. Write it correctly.

seechrc _____

owp _____

plurs _____

mobo _____

lckic _____

zzisel _____

chnucr _____

3. Homophones are words that sound alike when you say them but are spelled differently and have different meanings. For example, *see* and *sea* are homophones. Draw a line to match each pair of homophones.

knot   flew

break   soar

flu   not

sore   write

right   road

rode   brake

4. Add or subtract letters from each word to change it into another word. Write the new word.

peach – ch + r = _____

shirt – irt + oe = _____

sports – p – rts + ccer = _____

love – ove + ike = _____

chicken – c – ick = _____

brother – bro + nei = _____

Some names sound funny when you pronounce them backward. For example, Carol would be pronounced Lorac, and Jason would be pronounced Nosaj! Write your name and some of your friends' names backward. Are any of the names palindromes?

Best Friends

Amy dreaded recess every day. She did not have any friends to play with. All the girls in her class were paired up with a best friend or in groups, and she always felt left out. So, instead of playing with anyone, Amy just walked around by herself. She wanted to seesaw, but that is something you need to do with a friend. She liked to swing, but she could not go very high. She wished someone would push her to get her started.

One day, the teacher, Mrs. Gibbs, walked up and put her arm around Amy. "What's the matter, Amy? Why don't you play with the other children?" she asked kindly.

Amy replied, "Everyone has a friend except me. I don't have anyone." Mrs. Gibbs smiled and said, "Amy, the way to get a friend is to be a friend." Amy asked, "How do I do that?"

Mrs. Gibbs answered, "Look around the playground. There are three classes of third graders out here during this recess time. Find someone who is alone and needs a friend. Then go to that person and ask them to play." Amy said she would think about it, but she was afraid she would be too embarrassed. She wasn't sure she could do it.

The next day, Amy noticed a dark-haired girl all alone on the playground. She worked up her courage and walked over to the girl. "Hi! My name is Amy. Do you want to play with me?" she asked.

"Okay," the girl said shyly. As they took turns pushing each other on the swings, Amy found out that the girl's name was Ming. She and her family had just moved from Japan. She did not know anyone and could not speak much English yet. She needed a friend.

"Want to seesaw?" Amy asked. Ming looked puzzled. Amy pointed to the seesaw. Ming smiled and nodded. Amy was so happy. She finally had a friend!

Scholastic

On each blank, write the letter of the picture that correctly answers the question. One answer is used twice.

1. Where does this story take place? _____

2. Who is the main character in the story? _____
   Who are the other two characters in the story? _____ and _____

3. What is the problem in the story? _____

4. How does Amy solve her problem? _____

5. What is Ming's problem? _____
   How does Ming's problem get solved? _____

A. Mrs. Gibbs

B. playground

C. Ming needed a friend, too.

D. Ming

E. Amy

F. Amy asked Ming to play, and they became friends.

G. Amy needed a friend.

dove	record	live	lead	wind
dove	record	live	lead	wind

It rhymes
with **love**.

A **dove** is a bird.

A **homograph** is a word that is spelled the same as another word but has a different meaning and sometimes a different pronunciation.

It rhymes
with **stove**.

Dove is a past form of *dive*.

A band can **record** a song.
You can keep a **record** of your grades.

You **live** in a country.
A **live** flower is a living one.

Lead is a kind of metal.
If you **lead** a parade, you are at the beginning of it.

You must **wind** some clocks.
A strong **wind** can knock you down.

A. Read the words in each row. Circle three words that rhyme with the word at left.

1. live	hive	give	dive	five
2. lead	bead	head	bed	sled
3. dove	cove	drove	glove	rove
4. lead	bleed	feed	dead	weed
5. wind	find	grinned	hind	mind

B. Choose the correct word for each sentence. Write a or b in the blank.

a. rek′ ord   **b.** ree kord′

1. A thermometer will _____ the temperature.

2. The judge kept a _____ of the scores.

Some words are not spelled the way they sound. Some words have silent consonants. Sometimes two or three consonants are blended together to make one sound.

Say each word. Notice how each beginning sound is spelled. Circle the letters making this sound. Then make a ✓ in the box that tells where each object may be seen. Use a dictionary to help.

1. knob
- ☐ on a door
- ☐ on a window
- ☐ on the floor

2. wrench
- ☐ in a refrigerator
- ☐ in a toolbox
- ☐ in a sewing kit

3. cello
- ☐ at a grocery store
- ☐ at a post office
- ☐ in an orchestra

4. photograph
- ☐ on a CD player
- ☐ in a garden
- ☐ in an album

5. schedule
- ☐ in a classroom
- ☐ in a music book
- ☐ in a cookbook

6. gnu
- ☐ at a museum
- ☐ in an office
- ☐ at a zoo

7. wren
- ☐ in a jewelry box
- ☐ at a bird feeder
- ☐ on a workbench

8. gnome
- ☐ in the garage
- ☐ in the attic
- ☐ in a fairy tale

9. knuckle
- ☐ in your lunchbox
- ☐ in your body
- ☐ in your book bag

10. knickknack
- ☐ on a shelf
- ☐ in a freezer
- ☐ in a closet

11. ghost
- ☐ in a dishwasher
- ☐ in the sea
- ☐ in a scary movie

12. xylophone
- ☐ in a marching band
- ☐ in a kitchen
- ☐ on a desk

Think of words that end with *lf* as in *calf* and *lk* as in *talk*. Which letter is silent?

Piece of Cake!

Piece of cake *is an example of a common* **idiom**, *or expression. It means "an easy task." It is difficult to understand the meaning of the idiom by using the ordinary meaning of the words.*

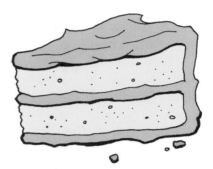

What does the idiom in each sentence mean? Circle the letter of the meaning that makes the most sense.

1. Jason was so tired that he *hit the hay* right after dinner.
   a. went to bed　　　**b.** went back to work　　　**c.** cut the grass

2. Do not waste your money on this video because it is *for the birds*.
   a. worthless　　　**b.** fantastic　　　**c.** expensive

3. Jasmine was *down in the dumps* after losing the game.
   a. smelly　　　**b.** excited　　　**c.** sad

4. "Rap music is definitely *not my cup of tea*," said Jack's grandmother.
   a. not cheap　　　**b.** not to my liking　　　**c.** not hot enough

5. Ben and Lisa do not *see eye to eye* about which movie to watch.
   a. agree　　　**b.** disagree　　　**c.** argue

6. "I don't recall his name," said Kim, "but his face *rings a bell*."
   a. is unfamiliar　　　**b.** stirs a memory　　　**c.** appears

7. Carlos has been *on cloud nine* since winning the contest.
   a. very unhappy　　　**b.** unfriendly　　　**c.** joyous

8. The two old men were sitting on the park bench *chewing the fat*.
   a. feeding the squirrels　**b.** having a friendly chat　**c.** eating lunch

9. Although he was losing by 20 points, Alex refused to *throw in the towel*.
   a. give up　　　**b.** take a shower　　　**c.** do laundry

10. I *kept a straight face* when I saw Ann's wild new hairdo.
    a. poked fun　　　**b.** kept from laughing　　　**c.** stared

Scholastic

Palindromes *are words, phrases, or sentences that can be read the same way forward or backward.*

noon	bib	kayak
eve	mum	race car
pop	dud	solos
pup	gag	toot

Write the missing palindrome from the box above in each sentence. Then reread each sentence. Can you find the other palindrome in each one? Underline the word.

1. It is a good thing you put a _____ on the tot because she just spilled her soup.

2. What did you think of the two _____ I sang at the concert?

3. Hannah taught her _____ to sit up and roll over.

4. My dad has to work until _____ this Saturday.

5. The soup Bob made was so bad that it almost made me _____.

6. "Would you care for coffee, tea, or _____, Madam?" the waiter asked.

7. Otto heard the train whistle _____ four times.

8. "You speed like a _____ driver!" Ava complained.

9. Refer to page 6 of your manual to learn how to paddle a _____.

10. Anna got the last ferry from the island on the _____ of the terrible storm.

11. "Keep _____ and do not say a word," ordered Mom.

12. Nan thought the movie was a _____.

Sometimes two words are confusing because they are similar in some way.

Read each sentence and question. Decide which underlined word correctly answers the question. Then write the word.

1. A package just arrived for Jason. Did he <u>accept</u> it or did he <u>except</u> it? _____	**2.** Sam had a sundae after dinner. Did he have <u>desert</u> or <u>dessert</u>? _____
3. Beth made a right triangle. Does it have three <u>angels</u> or <u>angles</u>? _____	**4.** All the actors sang and danced the last number. Did they perform the <u>finale</u> or the <u>finally</u>? _____
5. Megan swam the length of the pool underwater. Did she hold her <u>breathe</u> or her <u>breath</u>? _____	**6.** Aaron's socks slid down to his ankles. Were they <u>loose</u> or <u>lose</u>? _____
7. Jerome just made a dental appointment. Should he mark it on the <u>colander</u> or the <u>calendar</u>? _____	**8.** Lisa opened the gate and watched as the cows ate grass. Are the cows out to <u>pastor</u> or <u>pasture</u>? _____
9. Meg addressed an envelope. Should she add a <u>coma</u> or <u>comma</u> between the town and state? _____	**10.** Anna sketched a scene from a story she just read. Did she draw a <u>pitcher</u> or a <u>picture</u>? _____

 Are there any words that confuse you? Record them in a notebook. Include the definition and a sentence using the word. Think of ways to help yourself remember confusing words.

Scholastic

A **sentence** *is a group of words that expresses a complete thought.*
A **fragment** *is an incomplete thought.*

Write *S* for sentence or *F* for fragment.

_____ **1.** Insects eat many different things.

_____ **2.** Some of these things.

_____ **3.** The praying mantis eats other insects.

_____ **4.** Water bugs eat tadpoles and small frogs.

_____ **5.** Flower nectar makes good.

_____ **6.** Build nests to store their food.

_____ **7.** The cockroach will eat almost anything.

_____ **8.** Termites.

_____ **9.** A butterfly caterpillar.

_____ **10.** Bite animals and people.

_____ **11.** Some insects will even eat paper.

_____ **12.** Insects have different mouth parts to help

them eat.

Scholastic

Sometimes two sentences can be combined to make one sentence.

Sentences that share the same subject seem to go together like ketchup and mustard. Rewrite the sentences by combining their endings with the word *and*.

1. I ordered a hamburger.
I ordered a milkshake.

I ordered a hamburger and a milkshake.

2. I like salt on my French fries.
I like ketchup on my French fries.

_____

3. My mom makes great pork chops.
My mom makes great applesauce.

_____

4. My dad eats two huge helpings of meat loaf!
My dad eats two huge helpings of potatoes!

_____

5. My brother helps set the table.
My brother helps clean the dishes.

_____

6. We have cookies for dessert.
We have ice cream for dessert.

_____

Scholastic

Sentences can be written in order of beginning (B), middle (M), and ending (E) to make a paragraph.

Write a middle and ending sentence to complete each paragraph.

B **The circus started with a roll of drums and flashing lights.**

M Next,_____

E Last, _____

B **The tightrope walker stepped into the spotlight.**

M Next,_____

E Last, _____

B **The lion tamer came on stage.**

M Next,_____

E Last, _____

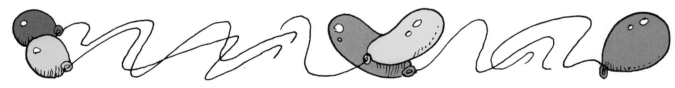

B **The dancing ponies appeared in the center ring.**

M Next,_____

E Last, _____

Scholastic

Present-tense verbs *must agree in number with the subject. The letters* **-s** *or* **-es** *are usually added to a present-tense verb when the subject of the sentence is a singular noun or* **he, she,** *or* **it.**

A. Read each sentence. On the line, write the correct form of the present-tense verb in ( ).

1. The crow ————————— the pitcher with pebbles. (fill, fills)

2. The man ————————— the crow. (watch, watches)

3. Then he ————————— the cabbage across the river. (take, takes)

4. The man and the goat ————————— the wolf behind. (leave, leaves)

5. They ————————— back on the last trip. (go, goes)

B. Write the correct past-tense form of the verb in ( ).

1. J.J. ————————— for the hidden picture. (look)

2. He ————————— at it for a long time. (stare)

3. Ana ————————— by. (walk)

4. Then she ————————— solve the puzzle. (help)

C. Write three sentences. Use the verb in ( ) in your sentence.

1. (play) ——————————————————————

——————————————————————

2. (plays) ——————————————————————

——————————————————————

3. (played) ——————————————————————

——————————————————————

Scholastic

*A **main verb** is the most important verb in a sentence. It shows the action. A **helping**
verb works with the main verb. Forms of **be** and **have** are helping verbs.*

A. Read each sentence. Circle the helping verb. Draw a line under the main verb.

1. Jamal had built his first model rocket last year.
2. He has painted it red, white, and blue.
3. Now Jamal is building another rocket.
4. It will fly many feet into the air.
5. A parachute will bring the rocket back to Jamal.
6. I am buying a model rocket, too.

B. Complete each sentence with the correct main verb or helping verb in ( ). Write the word on the line.

1. Kim _____ making a clay vase. (is, has)

2. The clay _____ arrived yesterday. (was, had)

3. I am _____ to watch her work. (go, going)

4. She is _____ a potter's wheel. (used, using)

5. The sculpture _____ go above the fireplace. (will, is)

6. People _____ admired Kim's beautiful vases. (are, have)

C. Write two sentences about something you will do later in the week. Use the future tense helping verb. Be sure to use a main verb and helping verb in each sentence.

1. _____

2. _____

Scholastic

Add or subtract. Connect the matching answers
to find each state's shape.

1.	Delaware	**16 − 9 =**
2.	Massachusetts	**7 + 7 =**
3.	New Hampshire	**15 − 6 =**
4.	New York	**17 + 1 =**
5.	South Carolina	**14 − 3 =**
6.	Maryland	**15 − 2 =**
7.	Pennsylvania	**14 − 9 =**
8.	Connecticut	**12 + 5 =**
9.	Rhode Island	**7 + 3 =**
10.	North Carolina	**13 − 7 =**
11.	Georgia	**7 + 5 =**
12.	New Jersey	**14 − 6 =**
13.	Virginia	**7 + 8 =**

a. 4 + 3 =

b.
9
+ 9

c.
7 + 2 =

d.
13
− 8

e.
6
+ 5

f.
8 + 5 =

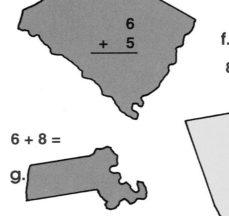
6 + 8 =

g.

h.
18
− 6

17 − 7 =

i.

j. 18 − 1 =

k.
15
− 9

l.
12 − 4 =

m.
9
+ 6

Scholastic

Add or subtract. Use the chart to color the picture.

white	blue	brown	red	yellow
0–20	21–40	41–60	61–80	81–100

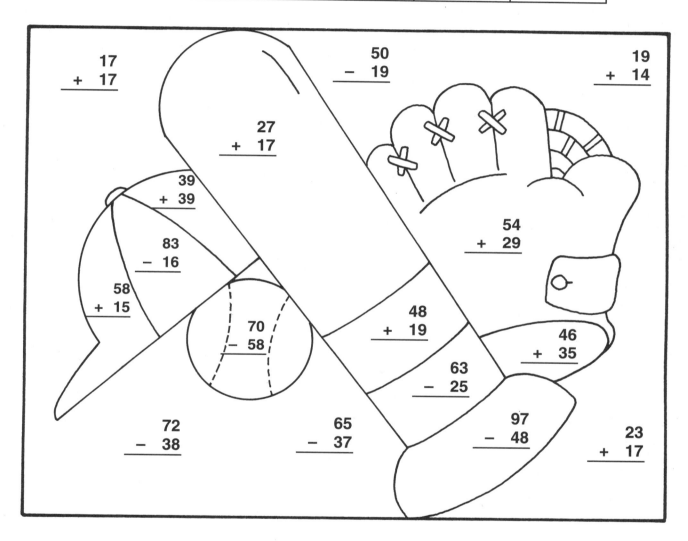

$$\begin{array}{r} 17 \\ + 17 \\ \hline \end{array}$$

$$\begin{array}{r} 50 \\ - 19 \\ \hline \end{array}$$

$$\begin{array}{r} 19 \\ + 14 \\ \hline \end{array}$$

$$\begin{array}{r} 27 \\ + 17 \\ \hline \end{array}$$

$$\begin{array}{r} 39 \\ + 39 \\ \hline \end{array}$$

$$\begin{array}{r} 83 \\ - 16 \\ \hline \end{array}$$

$$\begin{array}{r} 54 \\ + 29 \\ \hline \end{array}$$

$$\begin{array}{r} 58 \\ + 15 \\ \hline \end{array}$$

$$\begin{array}{r} 70 \\ - 58 \\ \hline \end{array}$$

$$\begin{array}{r} 48 \\ + 19 \\ \hline \end{array}$$

$$\begin{array}{r} 46 \\ + 35 \\ \hline \end{array}$$

$$\begin{array}{r} 63 \\ - 25 \\ \hline \end{array}$$

$$\begin{array}{r} 72 \\ - 38 \\ \hline \end{array}$$

$$\begin{array}{r} 65 \\ - 37 \\ \hline \end{array}$$

$$\begin{array}{r} 97 \\ - 48 \\ \hline \end{array}$$

$$\begin{array}{r} 23 \\ + 17 \\ \hline \end{array}$$

Finish the pattern.

32 34 36 ___ ___ 42 ___ 46 ___ ___

Scholastic

Multiply.

$$\begin{array}{r} 4 \\ \times\ 6 \\ \hline \end{array}$$

5 x 2 = _____

$$\begin{array}{r} 2 \\ \times\ 6 \\ \hline \end{array}$$

$$\begin{array}{r} 3 \\ \times\ 7 \\ \hline \end{array}$$

$$\begin{array}{r} 7 \\ \times\ 3 \\ \hline \end{array}$$

$$\begin{array}{r} 7 \\ \times\ 1 \\ \hline \end{array}$$

6 x 8 = _____

$$\begin{array}{r} 6 \\ \times\ 5 \\ \hline \end{array}$$

$$\begin{array}{r} 3 \\ \times\ 6 \\ \hline \end{array}$$

$$\begin{array}{r} 5 \\ \times\ 6 \\ \hline \end{array}$$

$$\begin{array}{r} 3 \\ \times\ 7 \\ \hline \end{array}$$

$$\begin{array}{r} 4 \\ \times\ 7 \\ \hline \end{array}$$

7 x 5 = _____

6 x 6 = _____

$$\begin{array}{r} 9 \\ \times\ 7 \\ \hline \end{array}$$

$$\begin{array}{r} 6 \\ \times\ 7 \\ \hline \end{array}$$

$$\begin{array}{r} 6 \\ \times\ 4 \\ \hline \end{array}$$

$$\begin{array}{r} 3 \\ \times\ 7 \\ \hline \end{array}$$

$$\begin{array}{r} 7 \\ \times\ 9 \\ \hline \end{array}$$

$$\begin{array}{r} 7 \\ \times\ 7 \\ \hline \end{array}$$

9 x 6 = _____

$$\begin{array}{r} 8 \\ \times\ 6 \\ \hline \end{array}$$

$$\begin{array}{r} 7 \\ \times\ 6 \\ \hline \end{array}$$

8 x 7 = _____

5 x 6 = _____

7 x 4 = _____

Color by using the following product code.

0–10 = purple   21–30 = blue   41–50 = yellow   61–70 = pink
11–20 = orange   31–40 = red   51–60 = green

Write a fraction for the section of the flag next to the arrow.

1. PANAMA
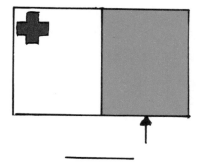

_____

2. NIGERIA
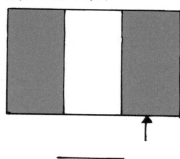

_____

3. TAIWAN
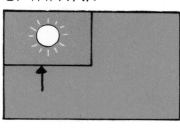

_____

4. MALTA
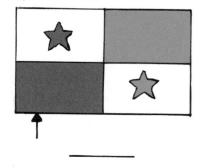

_____

5. POLAND
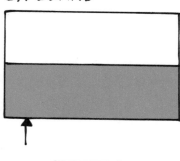

_____

6. MAURITIUS
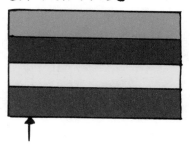

_____

7. RUSSIA
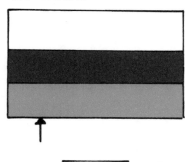

_____

8. CHILE
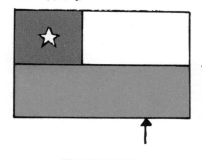

_____

9. MALAWI

_____

Read the riddle. To find the answer, find the clock face that matches the time written under each blank line. Then write the letter under that clock face on the blank line.

Riddle: What did the little hand on the clock say to the big hand?

Answer. "____ ____ ____ ____ ____ ____ ____
10:00 3:30 3:30 6:05 2:25 3:45 6:15

____ ____ ____ ____ ____ ____ !"
4:45 6:05 2:55 3:45 3:45 2:55

O U E N

T Y M A

Scholastic

Find the value of each group of money.

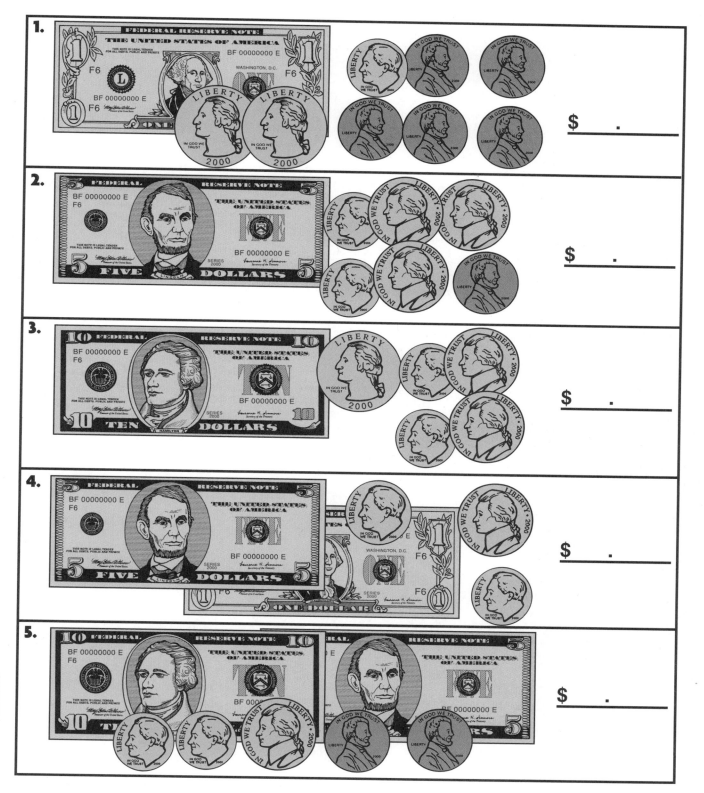

1. $ _____ . _____

2. $ _____ . _____

3. $ _____ . _____

4. $ _____ . _____

5. $ _____ . _____

Answer Key

READING/LANGUAGE ARTS
The Alphabet in Cursive

Page 14–39
Review tracing, copying, and cursive writing on each page.

Page 40–41
1. A 2. G 3. B 4. J 5. A

Phonics/Spelling

Page 43
bead, shake, let; wear, found, camp; should, ate, brush

Page 44
A. Three letters: map, ask, has
Four letters: last, sack, clap, mask, have
Five letters: after, black
B. 2. mask 3. clap 4. black 5. last 6. map
7. has 8. sack 9. have

Page 45
A. has, black, Last, have, ask, mask, map, clap, After, sack; B. 1. ask 2. black 3. last 4. after
5. has 6. sack 7. clap 8. have 9. mask
X wins 10. stamp 11. stand 12. backpack

Page 46
A. end with t: tent, met, went, nest, yet, best
end with d: send, bed, bend, said
B. tent/went, met/yet, send/bend, bed/said, nest/best

Page 47
1. tent 2. bend 3. best 4. bed 5. said
6. nest 7. send 8. met 9. went 10. yet
12. tent 13. met 14. bed 15. send 16. said
17. bend 18. yet 19. nest 20. went 21. else
22. bench 23. next

Page 48
A. begin with m: mix, milk, miss; begin with k: kick, kiss; have a p: tip, slip, pick; have an h: hid, with; B. 1. pick 2. milk 3. kiss 4. tip
5. slip 6. kick 7. hid 8. mix 9. miss

Page 49
1. hid 2. kick, pick 3. milk 4. with 5. mix
6. tip, slip 7. kiss 8. miss 9. sister 10. into
11. trick

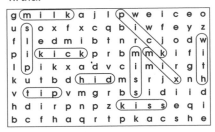

Page 50
A. rhyming pairs: spot/dot, box/fox, sock/lock, mop/stop; no rhyming partner: odd, off; B. 1. mop 2. stop 3. sock 4. fox
5. lock 6. spot 7. odd

Page 51
1. off 2. sock 3. mop 4. lock 5. box, fox
6. stop 7. odd 8. dot 9. spot 10. box, sock or lock 11. spot, off 12. box, sock or lock
13. odd, dot 14. stop, mop

Page 52
A. u: rub, bump, dump, must, dust, tub;
a: was; o: from; o_e: come, some
B. 1. some 2. must 3. rub 4. bump 5. was
6. from 7. come 8. dump, dust

Page 53
1. bump, dump 2. rub, tub 3. must, dust
4. come, some 5. some 6. was 7. rub
8. from 9. dump 10. dust 11. must
12. come 13. tub 14. bump Car on left wins

Page 54
A. no ending: tap, beg, skip, drop, run;
end with -ed: begged, dropped;
-ing ending: tapping, skipping, running;
B. 1. running 2. begged 3. dropped
4. skip 5. skipping 6. tapping

Page 55
1–4. Review sentences; 5. dropped 6. skip
7. skipping 8. run 9. running 10. drop
11. tap 12. tapping 13. begged 14. beg
clapped, stopping, tripped

Page 56
A. a_e: made, snake, trade, brake;
ai: pain, train, trail; ay: say, away;
unexpected: they
B. 1. say, away, they 2. pain, train
3. trade, made 4. snake, brake

Page 57
away, train, trail, brake, snake, pain, say, made, they, trade; 1. pain 2.A trail 2.D they 3. say
4. away 5. snake 6. train 7. brake 8. trade
9. made
1. raise 2. scrape 3. plate

Page 58
A. e_e: here, eve ee: meet, seen, wheel, sleep
ea: each, read, team, mean
B. 1. sleep 2. seen 3. meet 4. mean 5. team
6. read 7. here 8. eve 9. wheel 10. each

Page 59
1. week 2. team 3. here 4. each 5. wheel
6. sleep 7. mean 8. seen 9. eve 10. read
11. mean 12. seen 13. here 14. eve 15. read
16. sleep 17. wheel 18. week 19. each
20. team 21. easy 22. please 23. these

Page 60
A. i_e: time, wide, slide igh: right, night, light;
y: sky, cry, try, why;
B. 1. slide 2. try 3. night 4. right 5. sky
6. light 7. wide 8. cry 9. why

Page 61
1. night 2. slide 3. try 4. why 5. cry
6. wide 7. right, light, night 8. sky
9. time 10. stripe 11. while 12. bright

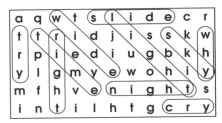

Page 62
A. o_e: nose, broke, close; ow: grow, snow, know; oa: toad, boat, soap, coat
B. coat, soap; know, broke; close, toad; snow, know, broke; grow, boat; nose, grow, coat; close, snow; nose, soap; toad, boat

Page 63
1. coat 2. boat 3. nose 4. broke
5. snow 6. toad 7. know 8. soap 9. grow
10. nose 11. soap 12. know 13. close
14. boat 15. snow 16. coat; Sled on right wins

Page 64
A. long a: snail, lay, game; long e: deep, meal;
long i: ride, might; long o: hole, blow, goat;
B. 1. blow 2. snail 3. game 4. meal 5. lay
6. ride 7. goat 8. hole 9. might 10. deep

Page 65
1–4. Review sentences; 5. game 6. hole
7. lay 8. meal 9. goat 10. deep 11. might
12. ride 13. blow 14. snail
became, globe, smile

Page 66
A. oo: room, food, moon, spoon;
u_e: tube, mule, rule, cute, tune;
unexpected: who
B. tube, cute 2. room 3. tune 4. who
5. rule 6. spoon 7. moon 8. food 9. mule

Page 67
A. 1. mule 2. cute 3. food 4. room 5. rule
6. moon 7. who 8. spoon 9. tune 10. tube
B. 1. who 2. room 3. moon 4. food 5. spoon
6. mule 7. cute 8. rule 9. tube 10. tune
11. scooter 12. goose 13. school

Page 68
A. ew: few, new, grew, flew, drew, threw;
ue: true, blue, glue   unexpected: two
B. 1. true 2. two 3. few, new 4. flew
5. blue, glue

Scholastic

Page 69
1. threw 2. few 3. drew 4. glue 5. two
6. new 7. flew 8. grew 9. true 10. blue
11. flew 12. glue 13. new 14. two 15. drew
16. grew 17. true 18. few 19. threw
20. blue 21. dew 22. due 23. knew

Page 70
A. u: put, pull, push oo: good, book, look, foot
B. 1. should 2. look 3. put 4. foot 5. could
6. good 7. pull 8. book 9. would 10. push

Page 71
1. pull 2. foot 3. would 4. look 5. push
6. book 7. put 8. good 9. could, would,
should 10. stood 11. shook 12. cookbook

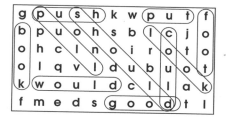

Page 72
A. sh: shell, shut wh: white, what
ch: chase, chat; th: than, them; wh and ch:
which
B. shell, wish; chase, them; shut, chat;
which, than; white, what; chase, what;
shut, than, wish; shell, chat; which, white,
them

Page 73
1. chat 2. white 3. them 4. shell 5. shut
6. which 7. than 8. chase 9. wish
10. shut, what 11. than, shut 12. what, shell
13. chase, them 14. white, wish
15. which, chat

Page 74
A. long u: tool, clue, blew; oo: bush, took
ch, th, wh or sh: thin, chest, shape, whale,
brush; B. 1. whale 2. brush 3. chest 4. tool
5. shape 6. clue 7. blew 8. thin 9. bush
10. took

Page 75
A. 1–4 Review sentences; B. 1. shape 2. clue
3. chest 4. took 5. tool 6. bush 7. thin
8. whale 9. blew; Answer to riddle:
automobile; shoe, choose, balloon

Page 76
A. Three letters: her
Four letters: bird, more, curl, were, hurt, your
Five letters: smart, sharp, first
B. 1. smart 2. hurt, her 3. first 4. were
5. bird 6. curl 7. sharp 8. more

Page 77
1. bird 2. first 3. her 4. your 5. smart
6. were 7. curl 8. hurt 9. sharp 10. more
11. sharp 12. bird 13. first 14. more 15. her
16. smart 17. hurt 18. were 19. curl O wins

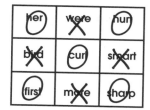

Page 78
A. ou: house, shout, about, count, our
ow: how, clown, down, now town
B. 1. shout 2. about 3. how 4. count
5. town 6. house 7. now 8. clown
9. our 10. down

Page 79
town, clown, count, down, our, shout, about,
now, house, how
1. down 2. our 3. clown 4. now 5. house
6. town 7. count 8. how 9. about 10. shout;
Clown on left wins.
11. found 12. mouth 13. crown

Page 80
A. oi: oil, join, soil, boil, coin, point;
oy: boy, toy, joy, enjoy
B. 1. joy 2. soil 3. toy 4. coin 5. boy
6. join 7. enjoy 8. oil 9. boil 10. point

Page 81
1. soil 2. boy 3. oil 4. point 5. boil
6. enjoy 7. join 8. coin 9. toy
11. oil 12. coin 13. boil 14. toy 15. boy
16. soil 17. enjoy 18. joy 19. join 20. point
21. annoy 22. voice 23. noise

Page 82
A. aw: jaw, paw, saw, draw, yawn;
all: tall, ball, hall, call, fall
B. 1. saw 2. jaw 3. draw 4. fall 5. call
6. ball 7. hall 8. paw 9. yawn

Page 83
1. paw 2. yawn 3. jaw 4. fall 5. tall 6. saw
7. ball 8. draw 9. hall 10. call 11. claw
12. hawk 13. dawn

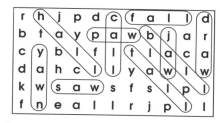

Page 84
A. vowel+r: art, horse, turn, girl, sister;
ou/ow: frown, south; all/aw: straw, small;
oi: foil
B. 1. art 2. foil 3. south 4. turn 5. small
6. sister 7. frown 8. horse 9. straw 10. girl

Page 85
A. 1–4 Review sentences.
B. 1. straw 2. turn 3. small 4. horse 5. art
6. girl 7. foil 8. frown 9. south 10. sister
Answer to riddle: an astronut;
purple, round, shirt

Pages 87–90
1. C 2. H 3. B 4. D 5. H 6. D
7. C 8. J 9. A 10. A 11. H 12. B

Vocabulary

Page 92
1. carrot 2. orange 3. food
1. broom 2. sweep 3. clean
1. flowers 2. leaves 3. smile
1. ducks 2. two 3. quack

Page 93
1. eggs 2. cracks 3. three
1. fish 2. bowl 3. jump
1. candle 2. flame 3. melt
1. boy 2. drive 3. wave

Page 94
1. zebra 2. stripes 3. animal
1. frog 2. tongue 3. fly
1. ghost 2. white 3. boo
1. turtle 2. shell 3. star

Page 95
1. frown 2. old 3. north 4A. left 4D. little
5. first 6. dirty 7. open 8. found 9. happy
10. across 11. stop 12. narrow 13. remember
14. smooth 15. tall 16. over

Page 96
1. pull 2. everything 3. empty 4. inside
5. last 6. play 7. cry 8. noisy

Page 97
1. small 2. outside 3. apart 4. leave
5. stand 6. worse 7. light 8. All

Page 98
happy; say; noisy; small; peek; big; afraid; set;
Synonyms are words that have the same
meanings.

Page 99
1. only 2. keep 3. forest 4. tired 5. happy
6. smelled 7. ripped 8. talked

Page 100
1. star 2. quarter 3. yard 4. down 5. rest
6. kind 7. train 8. jam

Page 101
1. dear, dear 2. to, two 3. son, son 4. cent,
scent 5. chilly, chilly 6. there, there 7. no, no
8. hare, hair 9. we, wee 10. hear, hear
11. wait, weight 12. brake, break

Page 102
1. shelf 2. hive 3. ground 4A. bath 4D.bed
5. finger 6. flower 7. lid 8. plane 9. brush
10. knob 11. farm 12. down 13. walk
14. cake 15. ball

Page 103

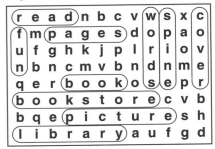

```
r e a d n b c v w s x c
f m p a g e s d o p a o
u f g h k j p l r i o v
n b n c m v b n d n m e
q e r b o o k o s e p r
b o o k s t o r e c v b
b q e p i c t u r e s h
l i b r a r y a u f g d
```

Page 104

```
W H A L E E T S Z C T F
L A S E P E Y H B X U I
O F D P R L V A N M R S
B G H O J K L R E K T H
S O C L A M I K U Y L T
T A S D O L P H I N E D
E S E A H O R S E G H F
R R D G J S H R I M P T
```

Page 105

```
g r a s s h o p p e r c
b w e r l a d y b u g r
e y b u t t e r f l y i
u i k m n a n t b f c
m o t h l j k u y s a k
r t e q a r o a c h o e
b e e t l e y s i m p t
n f h j m o s q u i t o
```

Page 106

square (red)   triangle (white)
rectangle (black)   cone (blue)
diamond (green)   cube (pink)
hexagon (purple)   oval (yellow)
cylinder (orange)   circle (brown)

Page 107

1. add, sum 2. subtract, difference
3. altogether, total 4. have left, how many
more 5. equal 6. solve

Page 108

1. anthers 2. petals 3. style 4. stigma
5. ovary 6. petals 7. stigma 8. anthers
9. ovary 10. style

Page 109

A. 1. head 2. thorax 3. legs 4. stinger
5. antennae 6. eyes 7. wings 8. abdomen
B. head, eyes, antennae, legs, thorax, wings,
abdomen, stinger
C. one million; beetle; atlas

Page 110

1. Australia 2. Asia   3. Greenland
4. Africa   5. South America 6. Antarctica

Page 111

1. responsibility 2. honesty 3. cooperation
4. consideration 5. patience; character

Pages 112

```
E A R T H K L Q N U W E
F R F G H J Q F E R N R
J U P I T E R K P A O P
M R S E W J L S T N Y L
A M E R C U R Y U U S U
R T D Y G U I O N S R T
S M V C X Z K A E A P O
S A T U R N M V E N U S
```

Page 113

```
s o l a r s y s t e m p
m m e t e o r j c k l l
o m o r t i l k o g m a
o s q w e r t k m y b n
n v s t a r s j e s n e
r o c k e t g h t u b t
a s t r o n a u t n v s
g a l a x y f d s a c x
```

Page 114

```
F I R E F I G H T E R D
A S D R E P W C Q T F O
B A K E R I M A L E A C
X C V B N L P P K A R T
C H E F O O I T J C M O
E R T Y U T Z A H H E R
D E N T I S T I G E R D
L A W Y E R J N F R A S
```

Page 115

```
d i f f e r e n c e s q
p w e r e g r o u p u b
l r t y u i o p l k b o
u z a d d f s g h j t r
s x c v n a s u m l r r
w b g e q u a l s u a o
a q m i n u s o h j c w
m a t h i f n d s v t m
```

Page 116

1. water 2. notes 3. drove 4. river
5. tame 6. month 7. awake 8. women
9. open, shut hard, soft

Page 117

1. climb 2. least 3. sour 4. see 5. brush
6. sad 7. full; baseball

Page 118

1. spin, turn 2. stairs, steps 3. friend, pal
4. pail, bucket 5. mad, angry

Page 119

1. B 2. C 3. B 4. A 5. C 6. A 7. B 8. A

Page 120

1. A 2. B 3. C 4. A 5. B 6. C 7. A 8. B

Page 121

1. B 2. A 3. B 4. A 5. C 6. A 7. B 8. C

Pages 127–128

1. B 2. F 3. C 4. B 5. H 6. B

Reading Skills & Reading Comprehension

Page 130

1. spots 2. seabird 3. a green stone
4. flute player

Page 131

Title: All About Our Alphabet
1. IOU 2. EZ 3. ICU 4. AB 5. TP 6. MT 7. IV

Page 132

Police officers help people

Page 133

On Saturday, Rachel got up early. Her
mom was still asleep, so Rachel made her
own breakfast. She put some peanut butter
in a bowl. She mixed it with a little *honey.
Then she stirred in some *oatmeal, *bran
flakes, and *raisins. It tasted yummy! When
Mom got up, she said, "Oh! You made
granola!"

```
B R A N F L A K E S M H N C L
O A T M E A L B K E Q O J W I
W R A I S I N S G R A N O L A
L G S A T U R D A Y P E R D R
G R A C H E L Y U M M Y F A H
```

Page 134

1. nap 2. Africa 3. fruit 4. wrestle
5. gorillas 6. sleep 7. chests 8. vines

Page 135

1. B 2. U 3. L 4. L 5. R
6. I 7. D 8. E 9. R 10. S bullriders

Page 136

Circle: cow; hay; tractor; calf; mud; ducks;
swam in the pond; pumpkin pie
X: pig; goat and sheep; horse; pizza and
hamburger; mouse; golden eggs; crickets

Page 137

R: a woman feeding animals; a house burning
down; a grandmother living alone; sleeping
on hay in a barn; crying because her house
burned down
F: deer that carry lumber; bears chopping
down trees; birds that can nail on a roof;
animals building a log cabin; a party that
lasted ten years

Scholastic

Page 138
1. math (underline "added and subtracted")
2. taking out the trash (underline "unloading baskets and cans into a large plastic bag", "took the bag out to the garbage can")
3. playing a video game (underline "put a cartridge in the player," "pushed buttons to make them move")
4. going to bed (underline "he put on his pajamas," "crawled under the covers")

Page 139
1. Mia begged Spooky to come down.
2. Mia asked Mr. Carson for help.
3. Mr. Carson called his firefighter friends
4. The fire truck came.
5. A firefighter climbed the ladder.
6. Spooky jumped to a tree and climbed down.
7. Mia scolded Spooky.
8. The firefighters laughed.

Page 140
1. his shadow   2. no
3. review child's opinion   4. review

Page 141
Color: 1, 4, 6, 7, 10, 11, 14, 15, 18, 20, 21, 24, 26 (teapot)

Page 142
People at Beach: Dad, Mom, Tim, Tara
Picnic: ham sandwiches, potato chips, apples, cookies, lemonade
Living Things at Beach: crab, stray dog, starfish, seagulls
What They Did: swam, fished, built sandcastles, went sailing

Page 143
1. cheerful/angry   2. away/west
3. goat/parakeet   4. mud/lemonade
5. toy/arm 6. Sarah/George
7. spinach/pudding 8. bicycle/crayons
9. marble/dime
Birds (3), Desserts (7), Bad Feelings (1), Boys' Names (6), Money (9), School Supplies (8), Directions (2), Body Parts (5), Drinks (4)

Page 144
(Accept any reasonable answer)
1. The home team wins the game.
2. The brownies will burn.
3. She will have a flat tire. 4. It will rain.
5. Mom will fall. 6. The boat will sink.

Page 145
Check drawings for reasonable predictions.

Page 146
Ryan: giant tortoise, three-toed sloth
Both: albino alligator Jessica: giraffe, owl

Page 147
1. both   2. Kendra   3. Lacey   4. Lacey
5. both   6. Lacey   7. Lacey   8. Kendra
9. Lacey 10. Kendra 11. Lacey

Page 148
The girls got too loud, so Dad said to be quiet. The girls saw a bee land on Dad's bald head, so Mary Beth whopped Dad on the head with a book. The car ran off the road and through a fence which let the cows out.

Page 149
1. spewing hot lava and ash into the air.
2. for people and animals to breathe.
3. flattened trees. 4. forest fires.
5. floods and mudslides.
6. it still erupts from time to time.

Page 150
Helping Others

Page 151
1. Man; Lady 2. hot dogs; chicken nuggets 3. frowns; smiles 4. Miss Daniels; Lunch Lady 5. hardware; shoe 6. mean; kind

Page 152
1. A 2. People loved the pandas.
3. letters from children expressing love for the pandas and how much they were missed

Page 153
1. D   2. coupons worth $300
3. It will take place on June 7.

Page 155
1. C 2. J 3. North Carolina's marshes
4. The Venus's flytrap senses an insect on its leaves. 5. The insect will be eaten.

Page 157
1. C 2. Brooklyn Bridge, Empire State Building, Statue of Liberty 3. France
4. The Statue of Liberty is across the harbor in front of you and behind you is an old fort you can explore.

Pages 158–161
1. C   2. F   3. C   4. B   5. J   6. D
7. A   8. G   9. C 10. A   11. G 12. D

Grammar/Writing
Page 163
1. T   2. Q   3. Q   4. T   5. T   6. Q 7. T
Page 164
1. fear 2. excitement 3. surprise 4. anger
5. Please don't be upset!
6. Review command.   7. Review exclamation.
Page 165
People: doctor, boy, aunt Places: village, office, school   Things: cane, pencil, bed
Page 166
1. George Ancona 2. Mexico 3. Jorgito
4. Coney Island 5. Honduras 6. Tio Mario
People: George Ancona, Jorgito, Tio Mario;
Places: Mexico, Coney Island, Honduras
Page 167
1. sandwiches 2. lunches 3. lunchboxes
4. dishes 5. boxes 6. dresses 7. coats
8. benches

Page 168
1. it 2. they 3. it 4. she 5. he
Page 169
1. runs 2. wears 3. smacks 4. holds
5. misses 6. waits 7. writes 8. helps
Review sentence.
Page 170
1. pushed 2. splashed 3. rolled 4. followed
5. washed; Review sentence.
Page 171
1. is; now 2. are; now   3. were; past
4. is; now 5. am; now   6. was; past
Page 172
1. present 2. present   3. present 4. present
5. past   6. past   7. past   8. past
Page 173
1. has 2. have 3. had   4. have 5. has
6. had 7. had 8. have 9. has
Page 174
1. donkey, brown; sack, heavy; 2. striped, cat; birds, two; 3. rooster, little; times, six;
4. brown, heavy, striped, little; 5. six, two
Page 175
2. "That's a great idea."
3. "What should we bring?"
4. "We should bring food."
5. "Yes, let's bring lots and lots of food."
6. "You're no help at all!"
7–9. Review sentences and check that quotation marks are properly placed.
Page 176
1. aren't; are not   2. doesn't; does not
3. can't; can not   4. couldn't; could not
5. didn't; did not   6. isn't; is not
7. hadn't; had not   8. don't; do not
9. weren't; were not
Page 177
1. writes 2. meets 3. ride 4. shop 5. closes
6. forget 7. locks 8. bang 9. call 10. hear
Page 178
1. new, newer, newest 2. small, smaller, smallest 3. warm, warmer, warmest
4. round, rounder, roundest 5. neat, neater, neatest 6. soft, softer, softest
Page 179
2. Sam's bowl 3. Emma's teddy bear
4. Dad's sunglasses 5. Fred's bone
6. Mom's hat
Page 180
1. noun 2. verb 3. noun 4. verb   5. verb
6. noun 7. verb 8. noun 9. noun 10. verb
Page 181
1. adjective (color box)
2. adjective (color box) 3. noun
4. adjective (color box) 5. noun 6. noun
7. noun 8. noun 9. adjective (color box)
10. adjective (color box)
Review sentences.

Page 182
Review sentences; check that commas are included correctly.
Page 183
Review that sentences have a subject, action, and a where or when.
Page 184
2. We blew up orange and red balloons.
3. We ate cake and ice cream.
4. The cake frosting was green and yellow.
5. We made a bookmark and a claypot.
6. We brought games and prizes.
Page 185
2. The first graders and second graders eat lunch at noon.
3. The napkins and the forks are on the table.
4. Are the muffins and the cookies in the oven?
5. Michael and Stephen bought lunch today.
Pages 186–189
Review that directions have been followed.
Pages 190–193
1. D 2. F 3. B 4. D 5. F 6. C
7. A 8. G 9. C 10. B 11. H 12. D

MATHEMATICS
Addition
Page 195

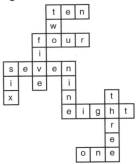

seven, nine
Page 196
1. 12 2. 14 3. 12 4. 8 5. 14 6. 16
7. 10 8. 17 9. 4 10. 6 11. 3 12. 12
13. 10 14. 15 15. 11 16. 6 17. 13 18. 11
19. 18 20. 15
Page 197
1. 12 2. 10 3. 18 4. 10 5. 13 6. 12
7. 10 8. 17 9. 15 10. 13 11. 11 12. 14
13. 14 14. 14 15. 18 16. 12 17. 16 18. 13
19. 9 20. 15
Page 198
1. 10 2. 10 3. 15 4. 12 5. 15 6. 14
7. 13 8. 18 9. 13 10. 16 11. 15 12. 15
13. 14 14. 14 15. 14 16. 14 17. 13 18. 13
19. 9 20. 15
Page 199
1. 13 2. 13 3. 14 4. 15 5. 10 6. 16
7. 10 8. 12 9. 18 10. 11 11. 9 12. 11
13. 14 14. 13 15. 12 16. 14 17. 15 18. 12
19. 10 20. 13

Page 200
1. 18 2. 1 3. 9 4. 2 5. 5 6. 6 7. 107
Page 201
1. 40 2. 8 3. 3 4. 2 5. 1 6. 80 7. 24
Page 202
2. 12 3. 16 4. 18 5. 14 6. 19
7. 15 8. 11 9. 17
Page 203
4 + 2 = 6; 7 + 7 = 14; 9 + 5 = 14; 10 + 4 = 14;
4 + 8 = 12; 6 + 8 = 14; 11 + 3 = 14;
14 + 0 = 14; 7 + 2 = 9; 13 + 1 = 14;
5 + 8 = 13; 12 + 2 = 14; 7 + 4 = 11; 5 + 9 = 14
Beans talk
Page 204

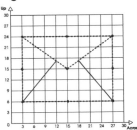

Page 205
21, 93, 78, 46, 44, 78; PLEASE
50, 67, 46, 79, 83, 59, 25, 66; THANK YOU
59, 25, 66, 32, 78; YOU'RE
80, 78, 93, 18, 25, 35, 78; WELCOME
Page 206
1. T. 38 H. 26 P. 97 R. 58 A. 67 E. 76 C. 79
2. E. 46 F. 84 O. 46 I. 89 U. 58 R. 48 F. 97
3. T. 58 I. 55 C. 65 H. 46 S. 40
4. Three-fourths 5. Pacific
Page 207
1. 69 2. 88 3. 45 4. 97 5. 25 6. 88
7. 45 8. 69 9. 25 10. 97
MATCH: 1 & 8, 2 & 6, 3 & 7, 4 & 10, 5 & 9
Page 208
75, 23, 98, 86, 47, 34, 75, 99, AMERICAN;
86, 98, 33, 78, 64, 87, 32, 47, 78, 99,
REVOLUTION; 64, 47, 51, 98, 86, 32, 21,
LIBERTY; 51, 98, 64, 64, BELL
Page 209
1. 71, 93, 90, 52   2. 92, 90, 91, 86, 92
3. 81, 81, 73, 42, 92   4. 85, 74, 92, 90, 94
5. 51, 41, 93, 81
Page 210
2 + 8 = 10; 24 + 7 = 31; 32 + 9 = 41;
1 + 9 = 10; 7 + 4 = 11; 45 + 5 = 50;
31 + 4 = 35; 11 + 9 = 20; 17 + 9 = 26;
22 + 13 = 35; 26 + 6 = 32; 19 + 9 = 28;
11 + 7 = 18; 16 + 22 = 38; 31 + 11 = 42;
14 + 9 = 23; 12 + 7 = 19; 40 + 14 = 54;
27 + 6 = 33; 12 + 9 = 21; 4 + 8 = 12;
41 + 21 = 62; 37 + 31 = 68; 16 + 6 = 22;
16 + 5 = 21; 10 + 24 = 34; 20 + 21 = 41;
15 + 5 = 20   Extra: Answers will vary.

Page 211
1. 21 2. 26 3. 14 4. 31 5. 35 6. 28 7. 27
8. 29 9. 58 10. 33
Page 212
A. 596 B. 995 C. 877 D. 569 E. 662
F. 978 G. 968 H. 596 I. 899 J. 497
Circle (Washington) – A, E, F, G, H
Square (Lincoln) – B, C, D, I, J
Page 213
35: 3 tens 5 ones, 2 tens 15 ones;
47: 4 tens 7 ones, 3 tens 17 ones;
82: 8 tens 2 ones, 7 tens 12 ones;
94: 9 tens 4 ones, 8 tens 14 ones;
61: 6 tens 1 one, 5 tens 11 ones;
90: 9 tens 0 ones, 8 tens 10 ones
Page 214

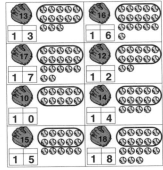

Page 215
2. 8 hundreds, 4 tens   3. 9 hundreds, 3 tens
4. 7 hundreds, 1 ten   5. 5 hundreds, 6 tens
6. 3 hundreds, 2 tens   7. 4 hundreds, 9 tens
8. 6 hundreds, 5 tens   9. 570 10. 804
Page 216
1. 40 tens 2. 20 tens 3. 70 tens 4. 50 tens
5. 10 tens 6. 90 tens 7. 80 tens 8. 30 tens
Page 217
15 + 33 + 27 = 75; 27 + 23 + 12 = 62;
34 + 23 + 24 = 81; 15 + 25 + 10 = 50;
16 + 14 + 14 = 44; 12 + 31 + 17 = 60;
28 + 22 + 45 = 95; 43 + 27 + 27 = 97;
10 + 17 + 18 = 45; 29 + 13 + 16 = 58;
37 + 31 + 17 = 85; 51 + 23 + 17 = 91
Page 218
A. Route 1: 13+48+88+39=188
Route 2: 13+48+32+54=147
B. Route 1: 13+17+31+49=110
Route 2: 13+28+10+25=76
Page 219
207 + 544 = 751; 126 + 89 = 215;
328 + 348 = 676; 257 + 458 = 715;
547 + 129 = 676; 624 + 127 = 751;
108 + 107 = 215; 229 + 418 = 647;
258 + 268 = 526; 379 + 336 = 715;
417 + 109 = 526; 153 + 494 = 647

Scholastic

Page 220

Page 221
A. $1.49 + $.50 + $.75 + $1.22 = $3.96;
B. $1.72 + $.65 + $1.17 = $3.54;
C. $1.86 + $1.84 + $.84 + $1.07 = $5.61;
D. $1.53 + $1.90 + $1.22 + $.84 = $5.49;
E. $1.86 + $.50 + $1.17 = $3.53;
F. $1.49 + $.86 + $.75 = $3.10

Page 222
A. 935   B. 690   C. 753   D. 779   E. 841   F. 768

Page 223
1. parties   2. 2   3. 10   4. 5   5. Matthew   6. 3
7. 24   8. school events

Pages 224–225
1. A   2. G   3. B   4. J   5. D   6. J
7. B   8. F

Subtraction

Page 227
Check that directions have been followed.

Page 228
1. 7   2. 3   3. 4   4. 9   5. 3   6. 3
7. 2   8. 7   9. 6   10. 8   11. 4   12. 2
13. 8   14. 4   15. 9   16. 2   17. 0   18. 3
19. 10   20. 6

Page 229
1. 3   2. 2   3. 3   4. 6   5. 5   6. 1
7. 5   8. 8   9. 4   10. 9   11. 5   12. 7
13. 9   14. 6   15. 3   16. 1   17. 5   18. 5
19. 6   20. 9

Page 230
1. 10   2. 9   3. 6   4. 8   5. 9   6. 9
7. 14   8. 8   9. 6   10. 5   11. 9   12. 8
13. 6   14. 3   15. 6   16. 6   17. 1   18. 9
19. 7   20. 9

Page 231
1. 7   2. 9   3. 9   4. 5   5. 7   6. 4
7. 5   8. 9   9. 6   10. 7   11. 3   12. 6
13. 7   14. 2   15. 10   16. 9   17. 9   18. 8
19. 4   20. 8

Page 232

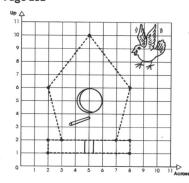

Page 233

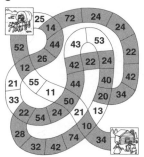

Page 234
1. 62   2. 33   3. 23   4. 30   5. 21   6. 14
7. 61   8. 22   9. 41

Page 235
2. 53   3. 70   4. 50   5. 65   6. 42
7. 71   8. 62   9. 44   10. 74

Page 236
54, 85, 43, 85; 43, 54, 67; 43, 67, 32; 32;
Check child's coloring.

Page 237
1. 43   2. 43   3. 2   4. 15   5. 21   6. 66
7. 3   8. 42   9. 33   10. 50   11. 33   12. 17
13. 30   14. 33   15. 12   16. 44   17. 42   18. 13
19. 34   20. 33

Page 238
1. 25   2. 23   3. 12   4. 21   5. 42   6. 50
7. 44   8. 11   9. 82   10. 26   11. 5   12. 31
13. 25   14. 14   15. 33   16. 22   17. 22   18. 43
19. 43   20. 10

Page 239
68 – 26 = 42; 34 – 11 = 23; 91 – 20 = 71;
47 – 15 = 32; 67 – 13 = 54; 88 – 54 = 34;
19 – 12 = 7; 33 – 21 = 12; 69 – 59 = 10;
88 – 12 = 76; 28 – 24 = 4; 17 – 6 = 11;
57 – 55 = 2; 27 – 5 = 22; 97 – 13 = 84;
35 – 11 = 24; 81 – 21 = 60; 39 – 15 = 24;
60 – 10 = 50

Page 240

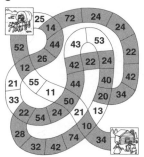

Page 241
2. 39; 39+38=77   3. 9; 9+15=24
4. 19; 19+13=32   5. 34; 34+49=83
6. 31; 31+19=50   7. 17; 17+29=46
8. 47; 47+15=62

Page 242
45 – 39 = 6; 84 – 59 = 25; 72 – 55 = 17;
71 – 19 = 52; 84 – 25 = 59; 60 – 18 = 42;
98 – 29 = 69; 74 – 15 = 59; 71 – 17 = 54;
88 – 29 = 59; 82 – 68 = 14; 91 – 32 = 59;
34 – 16 = 18; 92 – 13 = 79; 43 – 35 = 8;
57 – 28 = 29; She had 15 tickets left.

Page 243
A. 19, 39, 37 ; 1,3,2   B. 8, 6, 9 ; 2,1,3
C. 28, 37, 14 ; 2,3,1   D. 29, 38, 37 ; 1,3,2
E. 29, 36, 48 ; 1,2,3   F. 18, 15, 19 ; 2,1,3

Page 244
1. 9   2. 68   3. 7   4. 49   5. 48   6. 38
7. 37   8. 7   9. 39   10. 19   11. 39   12. 49
13. 68   14. 19   15. 9   16. 58   17. 28   18. 6
19. 29   20. 19

Page 245
1. 15   2. 39   3. 38   4. 46   5. 17   6. 8
7. 18   8. 5   9. 67   10. 14   11. 38   12. 47
13. 33   14. 29   15. 65   16. 8   17. 27   18. 49
19. 15   20. 28

Page 246
1. 19   2. 28   3. 58   4. 29   5. 9   6. 8
7. 19   8. 9   9. 6   10. 9   11. 18   12. 25
13. 19   14. 9   15. 19   16. 19   17. 6   18. 9
19. 9   20. 44

Page 247
35 – 17 = 18; 62 – 28 = 34; 53 – 14 = 39;
92 – 27 = 65; 82 – 23 = 59; 83 – 28 = 55;
67 – 48 = 19; 58 – 29 = 29; 72 – 17 = 55;
73 – 58 = 15; 42 – 26 = 16; 90 – 81 = 9;
52 – 28 = 24; 56 – 19 = 37

Page 248

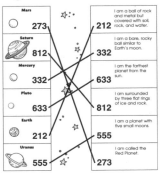

Page 249

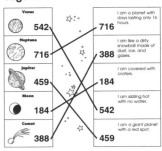

900, 800, 700, 600, 500, 400, 300, 200, 100;
Subtract 100.
900, 700, 500, 300, 100; Subtract 200.
800, 600, 400, 200; Subtract 200.

Page 250

Pages 251–252
1. B 2. F 3. A 4. C 5. J 6. B 7. F

Multiplication

Page 254

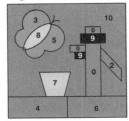

Page 255

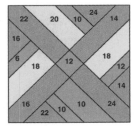

Page 256

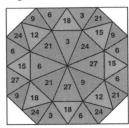

Page 257

Page 258

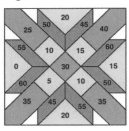

Page 259

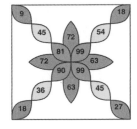

Page 260

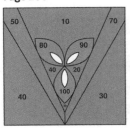

Pages 261–262
1. B 2. F 3. C 4. J 5. B 6. G 7. A 8. J

Time, Money & Measurement

Page 264
1. Eat Dinner 2. Come Home from George's
House 3. Eat Lunch 4. Go to Bed

Page 265
1. 1:15 2. 7:15 3. 2:45 4. 9:15 5. 8:45 6. 11:45

Page 266
1. 5:45 2. 4:15 3. 1:45 4. 6:15 5. 8:45
6. 3:45 7. 10:15

Page 267
1. 1:30 2. 5:30 3. 4:45 4. 2:30 5. 11:00
6. 9:45 7. 10:15 8. 8:00 9. 3:15 10. 7:30

Page 268
1. 25   2. 50   3. 50   4. 4 quarters,
2 half dollars   5. 6 quarters, 3 half dollars
6. 2 quarters, 1 half dollar

Page 269
1. 36 cents   2. 27 cents   3. 87 cents
4. 70 cents   5. 27 cents

Page 270
1. 62 cents   2. 71 cents   3. 37 cents
4. 82 cents

Page 271
1. a   2. b   3. b   4. a

Page 272
Answers will vary. Possible answers:
1. 2 quarters, 3 dimes, 1 nickel, 1 penny
2. 1 quarter, 2 dimes, 2 nickels, 2 pennies
3. 4 dimes, 3 nickels, 3 pennies
4. 3 quarters, 1 dime, 1 nickel, 4 pennies

Page 273
1. 2 quarters, 1 dime, 1 nickel
2. 3 quarters, 2 dimes, 2 pennies
3. 1 quarter, 1 dime, 3 pennies
4. 2 quarters, 2 dimes, 4 pennies
5. 3 quarters, 1 nickel, 1 penny
6. 2 quarters, 1 nickel, 1 penny

Page 274
1. 12:15 2. 3:37 3. 2:20 4. 7:27 5. 2:15
6. 11:20

Page 275
Answers will vary. Possible answers:
1. 2 dollar bills, 1 quarter, 2 dimes, 3 pennies
2. 2 ten dollar bills, 1 five dollar bill, 1 one dollar bill, 1 nickel
3. 1 five dollar bill, 3 one dollar bills, 2 quarters, 3 pennies
4. 4 ten dollar bills, 1 five dollar bill, 1 one dollar bill, 3 quarters, 1 dime, 3 pennies
5. 1 ten dollar bill, 1 five dollar bill, 3 pennies
6. 2 ten dollar bills, 2 dollar bills, 2 quarters, 1 nickel, 4 pennies

Page 276
1–4 Review that snakes of appropriate lengths are drawn.
X should be drawn on Snake #5 and Snake #7

Page 277
1. 1 in + 1 in + 2 in + 2 in + 1 in = 7 in
2. 1 in + 2 in + 1 in + 1 in + 1 in = 6 in
3. 1 in + 1 in + 3 in = 5 in
4. 1 in + 2 in + 1 in + 2 in + 1 in = 7 in
5. a   6. c   7. a

Page 278
1. Medium   2. Large   3. Large   4. Medium
5. Small   6. Large

Page 279
1. Mill Town   2. 3 miles   3. Maple Valley and Restful Hills   4. 12 miles   5. 3 miles
6. Restful Hills

Page 280
1. 3 + 3 + 3 + 3 = 12 units
2. 2 + 3 + 2 + 3 = 10 units
3. 4 + 2 + 4 + 2 = 12 units
4. 4 + 4 + 4 + 4 = 16 units
5. 2 + 1 + 2 + 1 = 6 units
6. 1 + 1 + 1 + 1 = 4 units
7. 1 + 4 + 1 + 4 = 10 units

Page 281
Review all estimates.
1. 9 cm   2. 5 cm   3. 10 cm   4. 6 cm   5. 8 cm
6. Review that directions have been followed.

Pages 282–284
1. D   2. F   3. C   4. H   5. A   6. J   7. A   8. H

GET READY FOR GRADE 3

Page 286
A. -er ending: swimmer, safer, freezer
-est ending: wisest, biggest, whitest
-ed ending: hoped, clapped, stopped
-ing ending: shopping, getting, coming
B. safer, wisest, hoped, freezer, whitest

Page 287
A. 1. biggest, check "double the final consonant"
2. hoped, check "drop the silent e"
3. coming, check "drop the silent e"
4. getting, check "double the final consonant"
5. whitest, check "drop the silent e"
6. wisest, check "drop the silent e"

B. 1. coming   2. shopping   3. clapped
4. stopped   5. swimmer   6. freezer   7. hoped
8. safer; Answer: cold medal
C. champion, medal, compete

Page 288
A. Review that directions have been followed.
B. Discuss child's choice of "tough" words.

Page 289
A. au: because, pause, sauce, author;
aw: hawk, awful, dawn, crawl;
augh: daughter, naughty, caught, taught;
B. Discuss child's choice of "tough" words.

Page 290
"c" spellings: office, excite, fence, center, since, price; "g" spellings: giant, giraffe, strange, gentle, danger, large
B. giant, gentle, large, strange

Page 291
A. giraffe, large, gentle, fence, center, danger, giant, strange
B. 1. large   2. office   3. gentle   4. strange
5. danger   6. excite   7. since   8. price
Answer: gigantic
C. monkey, antelope, elephant

Page 292
1. Alexander Graham Bell
2. a teacher of the deaf
3. "Mr. Watson, come here! I want you!"
4. Bell's assistant
5. Bell demonstrated his invention to people.

Page 293
1. circle: wow, dad, mom, noon, deed;
X: funny, tall   2. screech, pow, slurp, boom, click, sizzle, crunch   3. knot-not, break-brake, flu-flew, sore-soar, right-write, rode-road
4. pear, shoe, soccer, like, oven, hen, neither

Page 295
1. B   2. E; A, D   3. G   4. F   5. C; F

Page 296
A. 1. hive, dive, five   2. head, bed, sled
3. cove, drove, rove   4. bleed, feed, weed
5. find, hind, mind B. 1. b   2. a

Page 297
1. "kn"; on a door   2. "wr"; in a toolbox
3. "c"; in an orchestra   4. "ph"; in an album
5. "sch"; in a classroom   6. "gn"; at a zoo
7. "wr"; at a bird feeder   8. "gn"; in a fairy tale
9. "kn"; in your body   10. "kn"; on a shelf
11. "gh"; in a scary movie
12. "x"; in a marching band

Page 298
1. a   2. a   3. c   4. b   5. a   6. b   7. c   8. b
9. a   10. b

Page 299
1. bib   2. solos   3. pup   4. noon   5. gag
6. pop   7. toot   8. race car   9. kayak   10. eve
11. mum   12. dud

Page 300
1. accept   2. dessert   3. angles   4. finale
5. breath   6. loose   7. calendar   8. pasture
9. comma   10. picture

Page 301
1. S   2. F   3. S   4. S   5. F   6. F   7. S   8. F
9. F   10. F   11. S   12. S

Page 302
1. I ordered a hamburger and a milkshake.
2. I like salt and ketchup on my French fries.
3. My mom makes great pork chops and applesauce.   4. My dad eats two huge helpings of meat loaf and potatoes!   5. My brother helps set the table and clean the dishes.
6. We have cookies and ice cream for dessert.

Page 303
Review that directions have been followed.

Page 304
A. 1. fills   2. watches   3. takes   4. leave   5. go
B. 1. looked   2. stared   3. walked   4. helped
C. Review sentences.

Page 305
A. 1 had, built   2. has, painted   3. is, building
4. will, fly   5. will, bring   6. am, buying
B. 1. is   2. had   3. going   4. using   5. will   6. have
C. Review sentences.

Page 306
1. a   2. g   3. c   4. b   5. e   6. f   7. d   8. j   9. i
10. k   11. h   12. l   13. m

Page 307

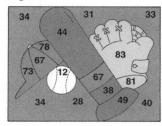

38, 40, 44, 48, 50

Page 308

Page 309
1. 1/4   2. 1/3   3. 1/4   4. 1/2   5. 1/2   6. 1/4
7. 1/3   8. 1/2   9. 1/3

Page 310
Meet you at noon!

Page 311
1. $1.65   2. $5.36   3. $10.55   4. $6.25   5. $15.27

SUCCESS with Reading & Math

You're a Scholastic Superstar!

has completed the
Scholastic Reading & Math
Grade 2 Jumbo Workbook.

Presented on

Congratulations!

SCHOLASTIC

SCHOLASTIC